Essential Elements

2-PART/3-PART VOICES LEVEL 1

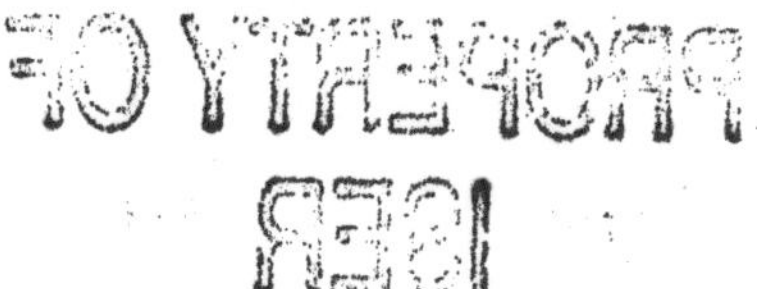

Developed by

Glencoe
McGraw-Hill

New York, New York   Columbus, Ohio   Woodland Hills, California   Peoria, Illinois

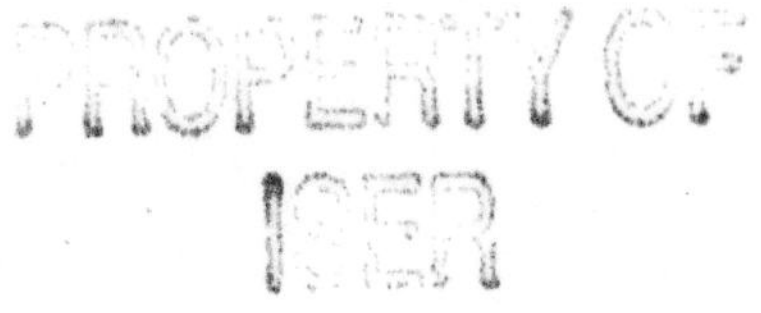

A portion of the sales of this material goes to support music education programs through programs of MENC—The National Association for Music Education.

Glencoe/McGraw-Hill
*A Division of The **McGraw·Hill** Companies*

Printed in the United States of America.

Send all inquiries to:
Glencoe/McGraw Hill
21600 Oxnard Street, Suite 500
Woodland Hills, CA 91367

ISBN 0-07-826037-X (Student's Edition)
ISBN 0-07-826038-8 (Teacher's Edition)

1 2 3 4 5 6 7 8 9 045 07 06 05 04 03 02 01

CREDITS

AUTHORS

Dr. Rene Boyer-Alexander, Professor of Music Education
University of Cincinnati, College-Conservatory of Music, Cincinnati, Ohio

Glenda Casey, Choral Director, Retired
Phoenix, Arizona

Emily Crocker, Vice President of Choral Publications
Hal Leonard Corporation, Milwaukee, Wisconsin

Dr. Rollo Dilworth, Director of Music Education and Choral Activities
North Park University, Chicago, Illinois

Bobbie Douglass, Choral Director
H. D. Bell High School, Euless, Texas

Cynthia I. Gonzales, Music Theorist
Presbyterian College, Clinton, South Carolina

Jan Juneau, Choral Director
Klein Collins High School, Spring, Texas

Dr. Janice Killian, Director of Music Programs
Texas Woman's University, Denton, Texas

Dr. John Leavitt, Composer and Conductor
Wichita, Kansas

Michael O'Hern, Choral Director
Lake Highlands High School, Richardson, Texas

Linda Rann, Product Manager, Essential Elements
Hal Leonard Corporation, Milwaukee, Wisconsin

Brad White, Choral Director
Birdville High School, North Richland Hills, Texas

CONTENTS

ROUNDS

Music Alone Shall Live **2**
Traditional German

Jubilate Deo **2**
Michael Praetorius

The Spring **3**
Traditional German

Viva la Musica! **4**
Michael Praetorius

Tumbai **4**
Israeli Folk Song

Come, Follow Me! **5**
John Hilton

Dona Nobis Pacem **6**
Latin Hymn

SINGING FUN

Make a Song for My Heart to Sing (2-Part) **8**
Julie Knowles

Cripple Creek (2-Part) **15**
American Fiddle Tune, arranged by Emily Crocker

Gospel Train (2-Part) **23**
Traditional Spiritual, arranged by Patsy Ford Simms

My America (2-Part) **29**
Henry Carey and Samuel F. Smith, arranged by Joyce Eilers Bacak

Antiphonal Gloria (2-Part) **36**
John Leavitt

SONGS OF THE GREAT COMPOSERS

Sleep, Gently Sleep (2-Part) **42**
Johannes Brahms, transcription by Ed Harris

The Loveliest Flower (Unison/Opt. 2-Part) **48**
Ludwig Van Beethoven, arranged by Emily Crocker

Come, Ye Sons of Art (2-Part) **54**
Henry Purcell, edited and arranged by Emily Crocker

MORE SINGING FUN

A-Rovin' (2-Part) 61
Sea Chantey, adapted and arranged by Emily Crocker

Hitori (2-Part) 69
Japanese Folk Song, arranged by Mary Donnelly and George L.O. Strid

Great Day (2-Part) 78
Traditional Spiritual, arranged by Rollo Dilworth

We Believe in Music (2-Part) 84
Kirby Shaw

SONGS FOR SPECIAL TIMES

Las Mañanitas (2-Part) 93
Mexican Folk Song, arranged by Audrey Snyder

Good Cheer (2-Part any comb.) 102
Based on a Medieval English Song, arranged by Audrey Snyder

Fum, Fum, Fum (2-Part/Opt. divisi) 109
Traditional Catalonian Carol, arranged by Audrey Snyder

Hanukkah, the Festival of Lights (2-Part) 115
Jill Gallina

SONGS FOR MIXED VOICES

De Colores (3-Part Mixed) 123
Mexican Folk Song, arranged by John Leavitt

Tinga Layo (3-Part Mixed) 132
West Indies Folk Song, arranged by Cristi Cary Miller

This Little Light of Mine (3-Part Mixed) 142
Traditional, arranged by Neil A. Johnson

Glossary 155

To The Teacher 169

TO THE STUDENT

Welcome to choir!

The reason students join choir are as diverse as the students themselves. Whatever your reason may be, this book was designed to help you achieve your particular goal. The many different types of songs in this book have been selected to fit your voice and allow you to be successful. In music, just as in many other activities, practice, effort, and dedication will pay off. Your study of choral music can develop skills that you will enjoy throughout your entire life. Best wishes for your musical success!

Student Expectations Checklist:

- Take responsibility for your own development as a musician.
- Every time you sing, make it a quality experience.
- Work to master the basic musical skills.
- Develop an attitude of wanting to improve every day.
- Be willing to try new things.
- Display an attitude of effort at all times.
- Come to class prepared to work and learn.
- Be present for all rehearsals and performances.
- Listen carefully during rehearsals. Critical listening improves the quality of a choir.
- Show a willingness to work with others.
- Choir is a "group" effort, but every individual counts. Working together is the key.
- Respect the effort of others.
- Practice concert etiquette at all times, especially during rehearsals.
- Make a positive contribution, don't be a distraction to the choir.
- Enjoy experiencing and making beautiful music.

ROUNDS

A *round* is a short, often unaccompanied song in which the voices, singing the same part, enter in turn at different times. Popular rounds are "Row, Row, Row Your Boat," "Are You Sleeping," and "Three Blind Mice." English composers have produced many *canons* and rounds, especially during the late *Renaissance* and early *Baroque* periods (1450-1650). Contests were held regularly to see who could write the best and most interesting canon. Many of these early canons and rounds are still performed today.

In preparing to sing the rounds, we suggest you try a variety of ways to learn them. Begin by learning to sing the round in *unison.* After everyone knows the song very well, let the teacher sing or play the second part on the piano or other instrument while the class sings the first part. Then divide the class into two sections of equal singing ability, and sing the round in two parts. After success with two-part singing, divide the class into three sections and perform as a three-part round. Experiment with different sections starting the round each time.

Use these rounds to learn how to sing in two and three parts. You may also use them as warm-ups before class rehearsal or a concert. Enjoy learning these fun songs!

Music Alone Shall Live

Traditional German Round

Jubilate Deo

Text from Psalm 65

Music by MICHAEL PRAETORIUS (1591-1621)

The Spring

German Round
English Words by MMH

Viva la Musica!

(Long Live Music)

MICHAEL PRAETORIUS (1591-1621)

Tumbai

Israeli Folk Song

Come, Follow Me!

Words and Music by
JOHN HILTON (1560-1608)

Dona Nobis Pacem

Latin Hymn

SINGING FUN

MAKE A SONG FOR MY HEART TO SING

Composer: Julie Knowles
Text: Julie Knowles
Voicing: 2-Part

Cultural Context:
Sometimes a song says things that we don't know how to say any other way. Julie Knowles has written the music and words to a song that speaks of thanks and happiness. These thoughts "make a song for my heart to sing." Read the words before you sing the song.

Musical Terms:

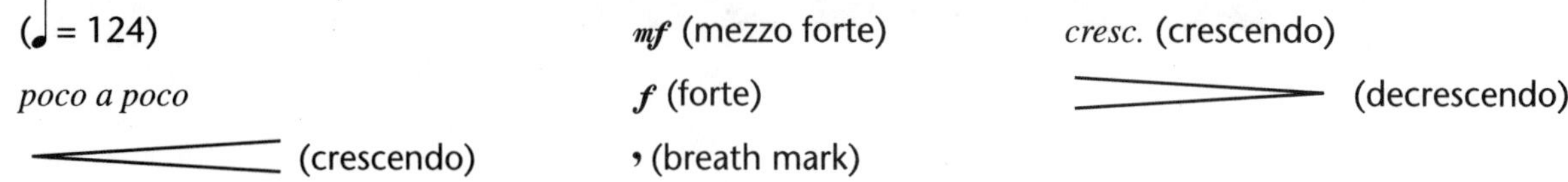

Preparation:
One of the challenges of this piece is holding long notes for full value. Practice this skill in the exercise below.

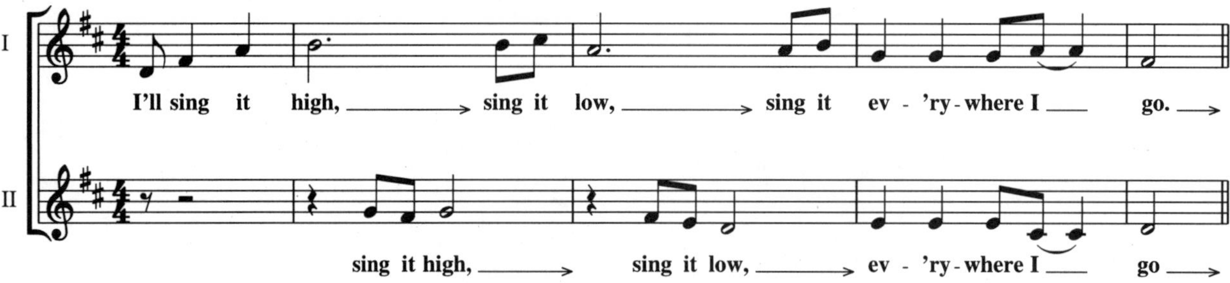

1. Practice the rhythm of Part I and II, and then learn the melody of each part.
2. Did you hold the long notes full value? Or did your voice fade before the next word?
3. Find every long note in this song (especially ones before you take a breath). Mark them with a pencil like the exercise is marked above. This will remind you to hold long notes for full value.

Evaluation:
After you have learned the pitch and rhythm of this song, do the following:

1. Part I, listen to Part II sing the first two pages.
   - Did they hold long notes full value?
   - Were there places they could improve?
2. Now switch tasks and answer the same questions.

Put both parts together and concentrate on holding long notes for full value.

Make a Song for My Heart to Sing

For 2-Part and Piano

Words and Music by
JULIE KNOWLES

9
cresc. poco a poco
take all my hap - pi - ness and love that it brings,_ and make a
cresc. poco a poco
take all my hap - pi - ness and love that it brings,_ and make a
cresc. poco a poco
9
f
13
song for my heart to sing.___ I'll sing it high, sing it
f
song for my heart to sing.___ Sing it high,
f
11
low, sing it ev - 'ry - where I___ go. Then
sing it low, ev - 'ry - where I___ go.
14

17
far, and_ wide, it's a feel - in' from in -
Then_ far, and_ wide, feel - in' from in -
17
22
mf
side._ How do you feel when the
mf
side._ How do you feel when the
mf
20
day is at end?_ Did you take time to be some - bod - y's friend?_
day is at end?_ Did you take time to be some - bod - y's friend?_
23

26
cresc. poco a poco
Think of the good__ times a new friend can bring,__ and make a
cresc. poco a poco
Think of the good__ times a new friend can bring,__ and make a
cresc. poco a poco
26
f
30
song for your heart to sing.__ Then sing it high, sing it
f
song for your heart to sing.__ Sing it high,
f
28
low, sing it ev - 'ry - where you__ go. Then
sing it low, ev - 'ry - where you__ go.
31

34
mf
far and_ wide, can't you feel it from in -
Then_ far, and_ wide, feel it from in -
34
38
f
side, in - side. What can I do at the
side,_ in - side._ What can I do at the
37
end of the day,_ to show my thanks in my own_ spe-cial way?_ I'll
end of the day,_ to show my thanks in my own_ spe-cial way?_ I'll
40

43
take all my hap - pi - ness and love that it brings, and make a
take all my hap - pi - ness and love that it brings, and make a
43
47
song for my heart to sing. And make a song for my
song for my heart to sing. Make a song
45
heart to sing.
for my heart to sing.
48

CRIPPLE CREEK

Composer: American Fiddle Tune, arranged by Emily Crocker
Text: Traditional with additional lyrics by Emily Crocker
Voicing: 2-Part

Cultural Context:

The days when a lone prospector might pan a fortune in gold nuggets from a Colorado streambed are long gone. But in 1890, a gold strike at Cripple Creek proved to be the richest in the state's history. This famous fiddle tune probably had its roots in the Appalachian Mountains. The early settlers loved to play the fiddle for any occasion. Alan Lomax, in his *Folksongs of North America*, states, "The fiddlers ... were rebels, bound and determined to get some fun out of life in spite of the disapproval of respectable folk!"

The arrangement of this famous fiddle tune by Emily Crocker was one of her first published pieces and is still popular with choirs today.

Musical Terms:

(𝅗𝅥 = 112-126)	*mf* (mezzo forte)	(tie)
𝄆 𝄇 (repeat signs)	*f* (forte)	*p* (piano)
mp (mezzo piano)		

Preparation:

Singing the words clearly so that the audience can understand them is important to the success of this song. Practice chanting these words in a whisper while exaggerating the movement of your mouth and lips.

Cripple Creek's wide and Cripple Creek's deep, he'll wade Cripple Creek before he sleeps.
Rolls up his britches to his knees, He'll wade Cripple Creek whenever he please.

Goin' up Cripple Creek, goin' in a run, goin' up Cripple Creek to have a little fun.
Goin' up Cripple Creek, goin' in a whirl, goin' up Cripple Creek to see his girl.

Halfway there he stops to rest, thinks about the gal that he loves best.
Picks him a watermelon fresh off the vine, spittin' them seeds sure do feel fine!

Evaluation:

One way to evaluate how well you articulate while singing is to view a video of your choir performing this song. Check yourself and other members of the choir for the following:

- The corners of your mouth are in, not out.
- There is space between your top and bottom teeth (jaw is dropped).
- Your lips move in an exaggerated fashion to clearly pronounce the words.

Cripple Creek

For 2-Part and Piano

Arranged with additional Lyrics by
EMILY CROCKER

American Fiddle Tune

from the tree,
Sweet-est lit-tle gal you ev-er did see.
p
10
13
Go-in' up Crip-ple Creek,
Go-in' up Crip-ple Creek,
Go-in' in a run,
13
Go-in' up Crip-ple Creek,
Have a lit-tle fun.
Go-in' in a whirl,
16

go - in' up Crip - ple Creek to see his girl.
go - in' up Crip - ple Creek to see his girl.
19
21
(clap)
(clap)
f
21
25
melody
f
Crip - ple Creek's wide and Crip - ple Creek's deep,
f
Crip - ple Creek's wide and Crip - ple Creek's deep,
f
25

mel.
he'll wade Crip - ple Creek be - fore he sleeps. Rolls up his britch - es
melody
he'll wade Crip - ple Creek be - fore he sleeps. Rolls up his britch - es
27
to his knees, He'll wade Crip - ple Creek when - ev - er he please.
mel.
to his knees, He'll wade Crip - ple Creek when - ev - er he please.
30
33
Go - in' up Crip - ple Creek, go - in' up to
Go - in' up Crip - ple Creek, go - in' in a run, go - in' up Crip - ple Creek to
33

have a lit - tle fun. Go - in' up
have a lit - tle fun. Go - in' up Crip - ple Creek,
36
Crip - ple Creek, go - in' up to
go - in' in a whirl, go - in' up Crip - ple Creek to
38
41
mel.
p
see his girl. Half - way there he stops to rest,
see his girl. Half - way there he stops to rest,
40

mf
mel.
p
thinks a - bout the gal that he loves best. Picks him a wa - ter - mel - on
mf
p
thinks a - bout the gal that he loves best. Picks him a wa - ter - mel - on
mf
p
43
mf
fresh off the vine, spit - tin' them seeds sure do feel fine!
mel. mf
fresh off the vine, spit - tin' them seeds sure do feel fine!
mf
46
49
1st time mp
2nd time p
Go - in' up Crip - ple Creek,
mel.
1st time mp
2nd time p
Go - in' up Crip - ple Creek, go - in' in a run,
1st time mp
2nd time p
49

go - in' up to have a lit - tle fun. Go - in' up
go - in' up Crip - ple Creek to have a lit - tle fun. Go - in' up Crip - ple Creek,
51
Crip - ple Creek, go - in' up to see his girl.
go - in' in a whirl, go - in' up Crip - ple Creek to see his girl.
54
57
Go - in' up Crip - ple Creek to see his girl!
Go - in' up Crip - ple Creek to see his girl!
f
57

GOSPEL TRAIN (WITH "THIS TRAIN")

Composer: Traditional Spiritual, arranged by Patsy Ford Simms
Text: Traditional Spiritual
Voicing: 2-Part

Cultural Context:

In this up-tempo arrangement, Patsy Ford Simms places two very well-known *spirituals* in a partner song relationship. In other words, these two songs are not only performed separately, but they are also performed simultaneously. The resulting harmonies, supported by a driving *ostinato* accompaniment, make this arrangement a delight to perform.

Musical Terms:

♩ = 160	spiritual	ostinato
f (forte)	*p* (piano)	*ff* (fortissimo)
cresc. (crescendo)	div. (divisi)	

Preparation:

Practice chanting the first two verses of "Gospel Train" as found in mm. 3-10 in your music. Be sure to carefully and accurately chant all the patterns. Clap to maintain a steady beat so that you can hear the syllables that are "on the beat" versus the syllables that are "off the beat."

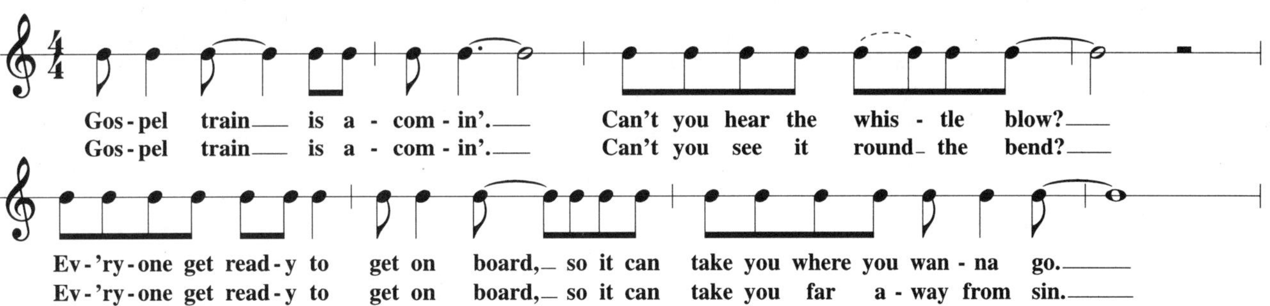

Evaluation:

As you learn this piece, answer these questions about your performance.

- Can you sing all of the rhythms accurately?
- Are you able to sing all of the dynamic changes in the score as indicated by the arranger?
- Can you distinguish between the passages that are syncopated versus the passages that are not syncopated?

Gospel Train
(with "This Train")

For 2-Part and Piano

Arranged by PATSY FORD SIMMS (ASCAP)

Traditional Spiritual

p
take you where you wan - na go.
take you far a - way from sin.
p
take you where you wan - na go.
take you far a - way from sin.
p
9
14
mf
This train is
This train will
mf
This train is
This train will
mf
12
bound for glo - ry, this train.
take all sin - ners, this train.
bound for glo - ry, this train.
take all sin - ners, this train.
15

This train is bound for glo - ry, this train.
This train will take all sin - ners, this train.
This train is bound for glo - ry, this train.
This train will take all sin - ners, this train.
18
22
This train is bound for glo - ry;
This train will take all sin - ners;
This train is bound for glo - ry;
This train will take all sin - ners;
21
you don't have to be rich to board it. This train is
get on board and you'll be win - ners. This train will
you don't have to be rich to board it. This train is
get on board and you'll be win - ners. This train will
24

bound for glo - ry, this train.
take all sin - ners, this train.
bound for glo - ry, this train.
take all sin - ners, this train.
27
32
f
Gos - pel train _ is a
f
This train is
f
30
com - in'. _______
Can't you hear the whis - tle blow? _
(whistle sound)
bound for glo - ry, this train.
Oo Oo. _
33

Ev-'ry-one get read-y to get on board,_ so it can take you where you wan-na go._
This train is bound for glo - ry, this train.
36
cresc.
Get on board the gos - pel
(whistle sound)
Oo Oo._
cresc.
Get on board the gos - pel
cresc.
39
ff
div.
train, hal - le - lu - jah!
ff
div.
train, hal - le - lu - jah!
ff
42

MY AMERICA

Composer: Henry Carey and Samuel F. Smith, arranged by Joyce Eilers Bacak
Text: Henry Carey and Samuel F. Smith, with new words by Joyce Eilers Bacak
Voicing: 2-Part

Cultural Context:

"My Country, 'Tis of Thee" or "America" as we know it today, is based on a well-known tune, the British national anthem called "God Save the Queen." In 1831, Samuel Francis Smith, a young American divinity student, wrote new patriotic words to the tune. He asked his good friend, Lowell Mason, to direct the first performance of "My Country, 'Tis of Thee" that same year in Boston, Massachusetts. One very important fact about Lowell Mason is that he is known as the first educator in the United States to add music to the curriculum in our public schools.

Musical Terms:

mp (mezzo piano)

mf (mezzo forte)

f (forte)

(crescendo)

(decrescendo)

descant

(fermata)

Preparation:

- The song "America" requires singers to sing in long phrases. You must sing six measures in one breath. Practice this at a slow tempo to build breath support:

- Now practice singing the first phrase of "America" all in one breath. As you build more breath support, you will be able to sing longer phrases in one breath.

Evaluation:

All by yourself, record yourself singing the first verse of "America." As you listen to the tape, decide if you are able to sing the opening 6-bar phrase in one breath. What other things do you notice about your singing voice? Try this activity again later in the year and then compare the two recordings. Has your voice changed in any way? How? Keep working to improve your breath support and singing voice.

My America

For 2-Part and Piano

America: Words and Music by
HENRY CAREY and SAMUEL F. SMITH

Edited and Arranged by
JOYCE EILERS BACAK

13
sing. Land_ of the free from
sea to shin - ing sea. My A -
mer - i - ca, let free - dom ring.
mf
mf
12
15
18
21

24
Part I
Descant
mp
Pur - ple moun - tain maj - es - ties, am - ber waves of
Part II Melody
mf
My coun - try 'tis of thee, sweet land of
mp
24
grain. This is my A - mer - i - ca,
lib - er - ty of thee I sing.
27
32
mp
of thee I sing. Land of the
mf
Land where my
30

free from sea to shin - ing sea.
fa - thers died, land of the pil - grim's pride.
33
mf
My A - mer - i - ca, let free - dom
From ev - 'ry moun - tain side, let free - dom
36
ring.
ring.
mf
39

43
mf
Our fa - thers' God to thee, au - thor of
mf
Our fa - thers' God to thee, au - thor of
mf
43
lib - er - ty, to thee, A - mer - i - ca,
lib - er - ty, to thee we sing.
46
no dim.
51
mf
to thee we sing. Long may our
mf
Long may our
no dim.
49

land be bright with__ free - dom's ho - ly light,
land be bright with free - dom's ho - ly light,
pro - tect us by Thy might, great God our
pro - tect__ us___ by Thy might, great_ God our
rit.
f
no dim.
King. My A - mer - i - ca!
King. My A - mer - i - ca!

ANTIPHONAL GLORIA

Composer: John Leavitt
Text: John Leavitt
Voicing: 2-Part

Cultural Context:
The texts "Gloria in excelsis" and "Gloria Deo" found in this piece come from the Latin Mass. The composer uses these texts in an antiphonal (echo) style in which one part often leads while the other part follows. The optional string bass and percussion parts make this work very exciting to perform.

Practice the pronunciation of the Latin text:

Latin: *Gloria in excelsis.*
Pronunciation: GLAW-r̃ee-ah een ehk-SHEHL-sees.

Gloria Deo
GLAW-r̃ee-ah DEH-aw.

r̃ = rolled or flipped r

Musical Terms:

poco a poco ritardando   ***p*** (piano)   ***mf*** (mezzo forte)

f (forte)

Preparation:

- Using the correction diction as indicated above, chant the following passage in rhythm.

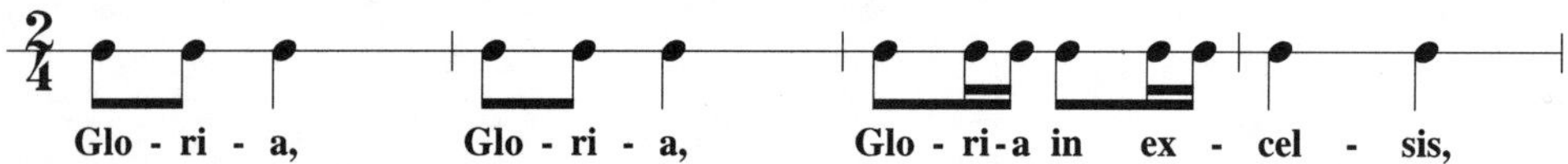

  – Put stress on the appropriate syllables.
  – Chant the passage at the dynamic level ***p*** (soft) and then ***f*** (loud).

- Look through your music and circle all the dynamic and expressive markings. Try to sing these markings as indicated by the composer.

Evaluation:
Listen to a class performance of "Antiphonal Gloria." Complete the chart below:

The choir:	All the time	Most of the time	Not very much
1. Sang all dynamics as found in score.			
2. Used good Latin diction.			
3. Made English words clearly understood.			

Antiphonal Gloria

For 2-Part and Piano

Words and Music by JOHN LEAVITT

13
p (energetic!)
And on earth good - will, peace to all the peo - ple.
p
13
(energetic!)
p cresc.
Glo - ry, bless - ing, a - do - ra - tion, Glo - ry, sing to God.
mf
mf
Glo - ry, sing to
cresc.
mf
17
21
Glo - ri - a, Glo - ri - a in ex - cel - sis!
God. Glo - ri - a, Glo - ri - a in ex - cel - sis!
21

Glo - ri - a,
Glo - ri - a, sing to God.
Glo - ri - a,
Glo - ri - a, sing to God.
25
29
p (energetic!)
For_ your_ great - est glo - ry, thanks_ and_ praise we of - fer you.
p
29
p cresc.
Hon - or_ bless - ing_ thanks_and praise,
mf
sing we to_ our_ King,
Sing we to_ our_
cresc.
mf
33

39
f
sing we to_ our_ King.
Glo - ri - a,
Glo - ri - a in ex -
f
King,
sing we to_ our_ King.
Glo - ri - a,
Glo - ri - a in ex -
f
37
cel - sis!
Glo - ri - a,
Glo - ri - a, sing to God.
cel - sis!
Glo - ri - a,
Glo - ri - a, sing to God.
42
47
p poco a poco. rit
f
Glo - ri - a De - o,
Glo - ry, sing_ to_ God!
poco a poco. rit
mf
f
Glo - ri - a De - o,
Glo - ry, sing,
sing to God!
p poco a poco. rit
mf
f
mf
47

SONGS OF THE GREAT COMPOSERS

SLEEP, GENTLY SLEEP (WIEGENLIED)

Composer: Johannes Brahms, transcription by Ed Harris
Text: Traditional German
Voicing: 2-Part

Cultural Context:

Johannes Brahms (1833-1897) is famous for songs such as this one, piano works, chamber music, and symphonies. He wrote during what is called the *Romantic Period* of music history. This time was known for expressive, emotional music which made frequent use of crescendos and decrescendos. Make many gradual changes in dynamics in this piece.

Brahms arranged this lullaby (*Wiegenlied* is the German word for "lullaby") as part of a collection of 14 songs. It was based on a German folk song which was probably well-known during his lifetime.

Brahms is one of our most famous composers. You will probably be able to find much information about his time, his life, and his music in any nearby library.

Musical Terms:

poco	*cresc.* (crescendo)	opt. descant (optional descant)
rit. (ritardando)	*poco a poco*	***p*** (piano)
pp (pianissimo)	***mp*** (mezzo piano)	Romantic Period

Preparation:

Balance between parts can be a challenge in this piece. Practice the following exercises to achieve an equal balance between Part I and Part II both when singing separate notes and when singing in unison.

1. Practice this exercise on a neutral vowel such as "ah" or "oo" until you can sing the notes correctly.

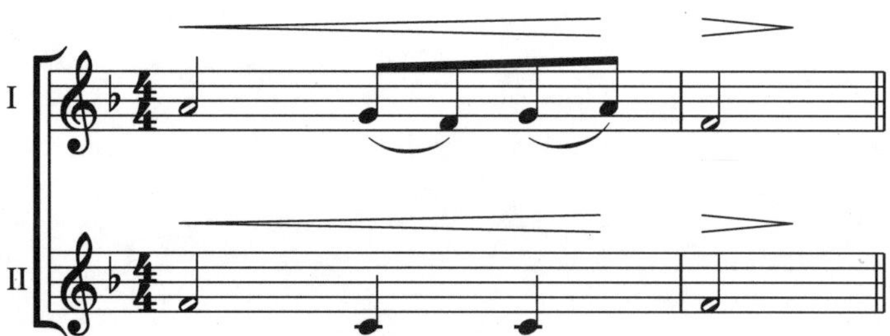

2. Practice again adding the dynamics. Make sure that you get softer at the end of each phrase. This may be difficult. Do you know why?

3. Circle the spots in the music in which Part I and Part II have the same notes (singing in unison). Your circles should be reminders that these are the spots that will need to be sung softer.

Evaluation:

After you have learned the pitches and rhythm of "Sleep, Gently Sleep" and can sing both parts easily together, ask yourself the following:

1. Is the choir singing each phrase with a crescendo in the middle and a decrescendo at the end?
2. Are the ends of phrases soft enough, especially where Part I and Part II have the same notes?

Sleep, Gently Sleep
(Wiegenlied)

For 2-Part and Piano

Traditional German, alt.

By JOHANNES BRAHMS (1833-1897)
Transcription by ED HARRIS

* If desired, the right hand accompaniment can be played an octave higher until measure 29.

sheep. They roam the heav'n - ly wil - der - ness, the
Schaf, die Stern - lein sind die Lüm - me - lein, der
sheep. They roam the heav'n - ly wil - der - ness, the
Schaf, die Stern - lein sind die Lüm - me - lein, der
mp
20
poco cresc.
p
moon will be their shep - herd - ess, sleep, gen - tly
Mond der ist das Schä - fer - lein. Schlaf, Kind - lein
poco cresc.
p
moon will be their shep - herd - ess, sleep, gen - tly
Mond der ist das Schä - fer - lein. Schlaf, Kind - lein
p
23
sleep.
schlaf.
sleep.
schlaf.
mp
p
26

29
Opt. descant
pp
Sleep,
Schlaf,
p
Sleep, gen - tly sleep, and I will give you a
Schlaf, Kind - lein schlaf. So schenk ich dir ein
p
Sleep, gen - tly sleep, and I will give you a
Schlaf, Kind - lein schlaf. So schenk ich dir ein
29
(loco)
29
p
sleep. The sheep will wear a gold - en bell and
schlaf, mit ei - ner gold - nen Schel - le fein, das
mp poco cresc.
sheep. The sheep will wear a gold - en bell and
Schaf, mit ei - ner gold - nen Schel - le fein, das
mp poco cresc.
sheep. The sheep will wear a gold - en bell and
Schaf, mit ei - ner gold - nen Schel - le fein, das
mp poco cresc.
poco cresc.
mp
32

poco rit.
stay with you 'til dawn's fare - well,
soll dein Spiel - ge - sel - le sein.
p
sleep, gen - tly
Schlaf, Kind - lein
poco rit.
35
p
sleep, gen - tly sleep, oh, sleep.
schlaf, Kind - lein schlaf, o, schlaf,
poco a poco rit.
mp
pp
sleep, sleep, oh, sleep.
schlaf, schlaf, o, schlaf.
sleep, sleep, oh, sleep, now sleep.
schlaf, schlaf, mein Kind - lein schlaf.
38

THE LOVELIEST FLOWER (DAS BLÜMCHEN WUNDERHOLD))

Composer: Ludwig Van Beethoven (1770-1827), arranged by Emily Crocker
Text: English Text by Emily Crocker
Voicing: Unison (Optional 2-Part)

Cultural Context:

Ludwig Van Beethoven, who was born in Bonn, Germany in 1770, is universally regarded as one of the greatest composers of Western music. As a young man, he went to Vienna, Austria where he met Wolfgang Amadeus Mozart and Joseph Haydn, and began to actively compose and perform. Beethoven was known to be eccentric, absent-minded, wild-tempered, gruff and rude, but the greatest tragedy of his life came around 1800, when he discovered he was going deaf. This caused him great personal suffering and grief, but he continued to write music. From the time he wrote his Third Symphony to his final Ninth Symphony, he never heard another note he wrote. He had to imagine the music in his mind. The story has been told that when he conducted the premiere of his Ninth Symphony in 1824, someone had to turn him around to see the wild ovation from the audience, for he could not hear the applause.

Musical Terms:

sempre ***p*** (sempre piano) **Andante** ***pp*** (pianissimo)

Preparation:

Articulation is the action of the lips, teeth, and tip of the tongue in making sounds. Practice the following exercise to stress the importance of good articulation.

Lips, teeth, tip of the tongue; lips, teeth, tip of the tongue; lips, teeth, tip of the tongue.

To practice speaking the German or English text, start slowly and then increase the speed. Articulate clearly. Try to memorize the text, making sure to articulate all consonants, especially at the ends of the words.

Evaluation:

With the help of your teacher, challenge yourself to learn at least one, if not all, of the verses of this song in German. Practice chanting the German text with a partner until you both can do it well.

The Loveliest Flower

(Das Blümchen Wunderhold)

For Unison (Opt. 2-Part) and Piano

Arranged by EMILY CROCKER

By LUDWIG VAN BEETHOVEN (1770-1827)
English Text by EMILY CROCKER

wird es Blüm-chen Wun-der-hold mit gu-tem Fug ge-nannt.
blos-som sure-ly is the lov'-liest flow'r in all the earth.
wird es Blüm-chen Wun-der-hold mit gu-tem Fug ge-nannt.
blos-som sure-ly is the lov'-liest flow'r in all the earth.
pp
13
sempre p
Wohl
Of
sempre p
Wohl
Of
3
3
sempre p
17
21
sän-ge sich ein lang-es Lied von mei-nes Blüm-chens Kraft, Wie
such a flow'r there tells a tale in mu-sic sweet and low, How
sän-ge sich ein lang-es Lied von mei-nes Blüm-chens Kraft, Wie
such a flow'r there tells a tale in mu-sic sweet and low, How
sim.
21

es am Leib' und am Ge - müth So ho - he Wun - der schafft. Was
day by day in grace and charm did mind and bod - y grow. No
es am Leib' und am Ge - müth So ho - he Wun - der schafft. Was
day by day in grace and charm did mind and bod - y grow. No
25
29
kein Ge - hei - mes E - lix - ir dir sonst ge - währ - en kann, Das
se - cret spell or po - tion can en - hance such beau - ty rare. Through -
kein Ge - hei - mes E - lix - ir dir sonst ge - währ - en kann, Das
se - cret spell or po - tion can en - hance such beau - ty rare. Through -
sim.
29
leis - tet, traun! mein Blüm - chen dir, Man säh' es ihm nicht an.
out the world one can - not find a flo - wer quite so fair.
leis - tet, traun! mein Blüm - chen dir, Man säh' es ihm nicht an.
out the world one can - not find a flo - wer quite so fair.
pp
33

sempre p
Ach,
A -
sempre p
Ach,
A -
sempre p
37
41
hät - test du nur die ge - kannt, die einst mein Klei - nod war Der
las! Could you have on - ly known the full - ness of my heart, But
hät - test du nur die ge - kannt, die einst mein Klei - nod war Der
las! Could you have on - ly known the full - ness of my heart, But
sim.
41
Tod en - triss sie mein - er Hand hart hin - ter'm Trau - al - tar! Dann
death was swift and death was cruel, we thus were torn a - part. And
Tod en - triss sie mein - er Hand hart hin - ter'm Trau - al - tar! Dann
death was swift and death was cruel, we thus were torn a - part. And
45

49
würd - est du es ganz ver - stehn, was Wun - der - hold ver - mag, Und
on - ly now I un - der - stand the truth in what I say, The
würd - est du es ganz ver - stehn, was Wun - der - hold ver - mag, Und
on - ly now I un - der - stand the truth in what I say, The
sim.
49
in das Licht der War - heit sehn wie in den hel - len Tag.
joy you brought in - to my life was like the light of day.
in das Licht der War - heit sehn wie in den hel - len Tag.
joy you brought in - to my life was like the light of day.
pp
53
3
3
57

COME, YE SONS OF ART

Composer: Henry Purcell (1659-1695), edited and arranged by Emily Crocker
Text: Unknown
Voicing: 2-Part

Cultural Context:

Henry Purcell (1659-1695) was among the greatest of English Baroque composers and organists. Born in London in 1659, he composed hundreds of musical works, including the opera *Dido and Aeneas*. Purcell also wrote a long series of welcome odes and other official choral pieces for King William III.

In literature, an ode is a lyrical poem frequently addressed to a deity. During the Baroque period, musical odes were longer works for solo voices, chorus and orchestra that were written to honor members of the royal family. Purcell wrote the ode "Come Ye Sons of Art" for Queen Mary, wife of King William III, on the occasion of her birthday in 1694.

Musical Terms:

mf (mezzo forte) *p* (piano) *rit.* (ritardando)

f (forte) (crescendo) (decrescendo)

𝄆 𝄇 (repeat signs)

Preparation:

The following exercise will help you to extend your vocal range and to sing slurs correctly. Sing this exercise using tall vowels like "zoh," "tah," or "loo."

Evaluation:

Answer the following questions:

1. As used during the Baroque period, how would you describe a musical ode?
2. For what occasion or "triumphant day" was this ode written?
3. Who do you think might be the "Sons of Art?"
4. Purcell lived and worked in what country?

Come, Ye Sons of Art

For 2-Part and Piano

Edited and Arranged by EMILY CROCKER

Music by HENRY PURCELL (1659-1695)

cel - e - brate, to cel - e - brate this tri - um - phant
13
1
2
f
18
To cel - e - brate, to
f
day. day. To cel - e - brate, to
f
16
cel - e - brate this tri - um - phant day.
cel - e - brate this tri - um - phant day.
19

f
Come, come, ye Sons of Art, come, come, a -
f
Come, come, ye Sons of Art, come, come, a -
f
22
26
way. Come, come, ye Sons of Art,
way. Come, come, ye Sons of Art,
25
come, come, a - way. Tune all your
come, come, a - way. Tune all your
28

voic - es and in - stru - ments play, to
voic - es and in - stru - ments play, to
31
cel - e - brate, to cel - e - brate this tri - um - phant
cel - e - brate, to cel - e - brate this tri - um - phant
34
38
mf
day. Tune all your voic - es and
mf
day. Tune all your voic - es and
mf
37

mp
in - stru - ments play, to cel - e - brate, to
mp
in - stru - ments play, to cel - e - brate, to
mp
40
cel - e - brate this tri - um - phant day, to
f
cel - e - brate this tri - um - phant day, to
f
f
43
46
rit.
cel - e - brate, to cel - e - brate this tri - um - phant day.
rit.
cel - e - brate, to cel - e - brate this tri - um - phant day.
tr
rit.
46

MORE SINGING FUN

A-ROVIN'

Composer: Sea Chantey, adapted and arranged by Emily Crocker
Text: Traditional
Voicing: 2-Part

Cultural Context:
A *chantey* is a work song sung by merchant sailors. Singing together allows a crew to synchronize the strenuous tasks required to sail a ship, such as hauling the sails, heaving the anchor, and pumping out the ship. The oldest known chanties are simple cries that would coordinate work activities, so that the sailors would haul, heave, or pump together. Over time, chanties developed into songs that told a story. Both older and newer styles typically featured alternation between a lead singer, known as a "shanteyman," and the chorus of sailors.

Musical Terms:

𝅗𝅥 = 100	***f*** (forte)	***mf*** (mezzo forte)
rit. (ritardando)	***mp*** (mezzo piano)	𝄆 𝄇 (repeat signs)
𝅗𝅥. = 52	**Tempo Primo**	*molto rit.* (molto ritardando)
> (accent)	𝄐 (fermata)	chantey

Preparation:
The time signature for "A-Rovin'" is cut time, which is 2/2, often shown as ¢.
Scan the music. You'll notice that rhythms written in 2/2 look the same as those in 4/4, also known as common time. Although these time signatures may look the same, they sound different.

Cut Time	Common Time
2 beats per measure	4 beats per measure
stress on downbeat (one stress per measure)	primary stress on downbeat and secondary stress on third quarter note

Evaluation:
- After you have learned "A-Rovin'," record yourself singing your part. Listen to the recording.
  - Do you hear one stress per measure on the downbeat?
  - Are you singing with tall vowels?
  - Is your diction clear?
  - Can you hear both parts clearly with one part not overpowering the other?
  - Does your performance express the mood and meaning of the song?
- Keep practicing until you can honestly say "yes" to all these things when you sing this song.

A-Rovin'

For 2-Part and Piano

Adapted and Arranged by EMILY CROCKER

Sea Chantey

sai - lor stayed.
love - ly talk.
I'll rove no more with you, fair
I will go no more a - rov - in' with you, my fair
13
maid. A - rov - in', a - rov - in', since rov - in's been my
maid. A - rov - in', a - rov - in'.
18
17
ru - i - in.* I'll rove no more with
I'll go no more a - rov - in' with
21

* roo - eye - in

1
2
you, fair maid.
maid. And
you, my fair___ maid.
maid. And
24
27
mf
he did tell her sto - ries true, mark well what I do say. And
mf
he did tell her sto - ries true, mark well what I do say. And
mf
27
he did tell her sto - ries true of the gold they found in Tim - buk - tu.
he did tell her sto - ries true. And I___ will___
31

f
I'll rove no more with you, fair maid. A -
go no more a - rov - in' with you, my fair maid.
35
39
rov - in', a - rov - in', since rov - in's been my ru - i - in.
f
A - rov - in', a - rov - in', I'll
f
39
I'll rove no more with you, fair maid.
go no more a - rov - in' with you my fair maid.
mp
43

47
molto rit.
♩. = 52
mp
But
molto rit.
mp
But
molto rit.
mp
47
52
when his cash was gone and spent, mark
when his cash was gone and spent, mark
52
mf
well what I do say.
Solo
mf
well what I do say.
But
mf
56

Freely
when my cash was gone and spent, then
64 Tempo Primo
I'll rove no more with
All
this fair maid a - way she went I'll go no more a - rov - in' with
you fair maid. A - rov - in', a - rov - in', since
70
you my fair maid. A - rov - in', a - rov - in'.

rov - in's been my ru - i - in. I'll
I'll go no more a -
72
rove no more with you, fair maid. I'll go no more a -
rov - in' with you, my fair maid. I'll go no more a -
f
75
rit.
mp
rov - in' with you fair maid!
rov - in' with you fair maid!
79

HITORI (HERE AM I)

Composer: Japanese Folk Song, arranged by Mary Donnelly and George L.O. Strid
Text: Traditional Japanese with additional lyrics by Mary Donnelly and George L.O. Strid
Voicing: 2-Part

Cultural Context:
As you read the English adaptation of the Japanese text, you will discover that it expresses a view of an individual who yearns to return home.

Here am I, so all alone dreaming of the cherry trees of home.

There by the river sits a pretty maiden
Watching the water move along.
She sees a lovely blossoming cherry tree
And her heart is filled with song.
"Some day I will go to my home that I love so.
Once more I will be 'neath the lovely cherry tree."

Here am I, so all alone dreaming of the cherry trees of home.

Now as the moonlight dances on the river,
Sadly the maiden must depart.
Each gentle breeze that sighs through the cherry tree
Echoes the song that fills her heart.
"Some day I will go to my home that I love so.
Once more I will be 'neath the lovely cherry tree."

Here am I, so all alone dreaming of the cherry trees of home.

Musical Terms:

mp (mezzo piano)	canon	*mf* (mezzo forte)
drone/bourdon	div. (divisi)	

Preparation:
Practice the Japanese pronunciation:

Japanese:	*Hitori de sabishii,*
Pronunciation:	hee-toh-ree day sah-bee-shee
	Futari de mairima sho.
	foo-tah-ree day mah-ee-ree-mah shohw

Evaluation:
To evaluate how well you are able to perform "Hitori," check the following:
- I sang with tall, pure vowels.
- My vowel sounds blended with the other singers around me.
- Through my singing, I was able to express the emotion and style of the piece.
- I was able to stay on my part during the canon in mm. 57-66.

Hitori

For 2-Part and Piano with Orff Instruments

Additional Lyrics and Arrangement by
MARY DONNELLY (ASCAP) and GEORGE L.O. STRID (ASCAP)

Japanese Folk Song

*Orff instruments double piano part, so song may be sung with or without piano.
(Wind Chime, Bass Xylophone, Alto Xylophone, Finger Cymbal, Soprano Glockenspiel)
**English lyrics optional.
Japanese pronunciations:
Hee-toh-ree day sah-bee-shee
Foo-tah-ree day mah-ee-ree mah show

Hi - to - ri de sa - bi - shii, Fu - ta - ri de
Here am I, so all a - lone dream - ing of the
15

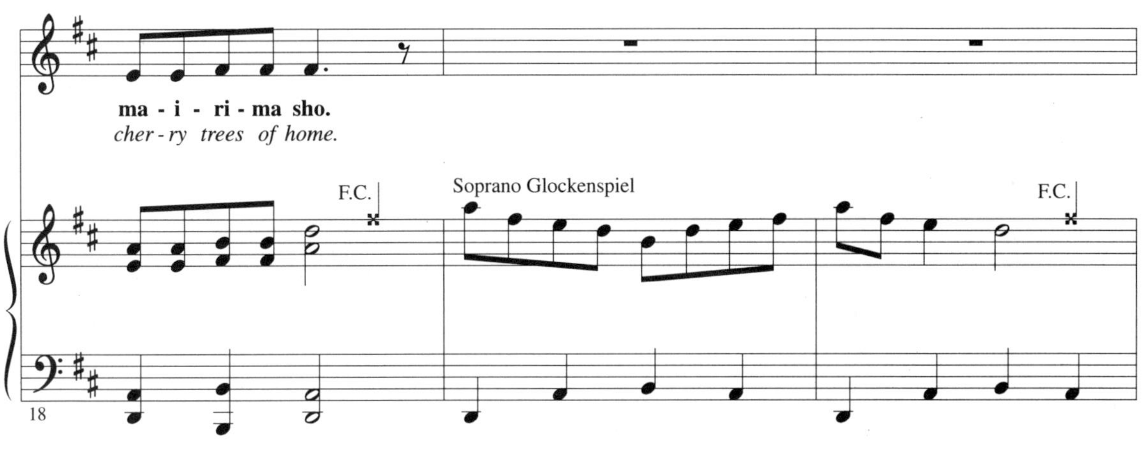
ma - i - ri - ma sho.
cher - ry trees of home.
F.C.
Soprano Glockenspiel
F.C.
18

21
Part I
mp
There by the riv - er sits a pret - ty maid - en watch - ing the wa - ter
mp
Part II
div.
Slow - ly mov - ing. Mov - ing
21

move a - long. She sees a love - ly blos - som-ing cher-ry tree
slow. Slow - ly mov - ing.
F.C.
24
29
and her heart is filled with song. "Some - day
Mov - ing slow. "Some - day
F.C.
27
I will go to my home that I love so.
I will go to my home that I love so.
30

Once more I will be 'neath the love - ly
Once more I will be 'neath the love - ly
33
cher - ry tree."
cher - ry tree."
Alto Xylophone
36
39
Hi - to - ri de sa - bi - shii, Fu - ta - ri de
Here am I, so all a - lone dream - ing of the
Hi - to - ri de sa - bi - shii, Fu - ta - ri de
Here am I, so all a - lone dream - ing of the
39

ma - i - ri - ma sho. Hi - to - ri de sa - bi - shii,
cher - ry trees of home. Here am___ I, so all a - lone
ma - i - ri - ma sho. Hi - to - ri de sa - bi - shii,
cher - ry trees of home. Here am___ I, so all a - lone
F.C.
42
Fu - ta - ri de ma - i - ri - ma sho.
dream - ing of the cher - ry trees of home.
Fu - ta - ri de ma - i - ri - ma sho.
dream - ing of the cher - ry trees of home.
F.C.
Soprano Glockenspiel
45
49
mf
Now, as the moon - light dan - ces on the riv - er,
F.C.
mf
48

sad - ly the maid - en must de - part.
mf
Each gen-tle breeze that
F.C.
51
sighs_ through the cher - ry tree ech - oes the song that fills her heart.
F.C.
54
57
"Some - day I will_ go to my home that
"Some - day I will_ go
57

I love so. Once more I will be
to my home that I love so. Once more
60
'neath the love - ly cher - ry tree."
I will be 'neath the love - ly cher - ry
Alto Xylophone
63
67
mp
Hi - to - ri de sa - bi - shii,
Here am I, so all a - lone
tree."
Hi - to - ri de sa - bi - shii,
Here am I, so all a - lone
66

Fu - ta - ri de ma - i - ri - ma sho. Hi - to - ri de
dream - ing of the cher - ry trees of home. Here am I, so
Fu - ta - ri de ma - i - ri - ma sho. Hi - to - ri de
dream - ing of the cher - ry trees of home. Here am I, so
F.C.
69
sa - bi - shii, Fu - ta - ri de ma - i - ri - ma
all a - lone dream - ing of the cher - ry trees of
sa - bi - shii, Fu - ta - ri de ma - i - ri - ma
all a - lone dream - ing of the cher - ry trees of
72
sho.
home.
sho.
home.
Wind Chime
75

GREAT DAY!

Composer: Traditional Spiritual, arranged by Rollo Dilworth
Text: Traditional Spiritual
Voicing: 2-Part

Cultural Context:
"Great Day!," like many traditional *spirituals,* is a jubilant expression of joy for the freedom and social justice which is to come. The arrangement begins with the chorus in its original form (A section). The verses of the spiritual are set in a *call and response* format (B section). The chorus returns at the end of the piece in an improvised form that features *syncopated* rhythms and *blue notes.*

Musical Terms:

spiritual	*sub.* (subito)	Poco allargando
call and response	**A Tempo**	syncopation
blue notes	*cresc. e. accel.* (crescendo and accelerando)	

Preparation:
Chant the opening chorus of this arrangement in rhythm.

Once you are successful at chanting the words in rhythm, try the following:

- March in place or around the classroom while chanting.
- Learn the pitches of the passage and sing the melody as you march. Be sure to sing in a style that is majestic and lively.

Evaluation:
As you perform the piece, listen for clear diction as you sing in a lively manner. Also, try to identify the call and response patterns as well as the blue notes in the arrangement.

Great Day

For 2-Part and Piano

Arranged by ROLLO A. DILWORTH

Traditional Spiritual

7
mp
Great day! Great day, the right - eous march - in'.
mp
Great day! Great day, the right - eous march - in'.
mp
7
sub. f
Great day! God's a - gon - na build up Zi - on's walls. Char-
We
Great day! God's a - gon - na build up Zi - on's walls.
sub. f
9
11
- iot rode in the moun - tain top. My
want no cow - ards in our band. As
mf
God's a - gon - na build up Zi - on's walls.
11

God spoke and the char - iot did stop.
we go march - in' through the land.
sub. f
God's a - gon - na build up Zi - on's walls. This
I'll
13
15
mf
God's a - gon - na build up Zi - on's walls.
is the day of ju - bi - lee.
take my breast - plate, sword and shield.
The
And
15
f
God's a - gon - na build up Zi - on's walls.
Lord has set His peo - ple free.
march out bold - ly in the field.
17

19
Great day! Great day, the right-eous march-in'.
Great day, oh great day! Great day, the right-eous march-in'.
19
Great day! God's a-gon-na build up Zi-on's walls.
Great day, great day! God's gon-na build up,
21
23
Great day! Great day, the right-eous march-in'.
in that great day! Great day, the right-eous march-in'.
23

26
Poco allargando
Broaden
cresc. e accelerando
div.
mp
Great___ day! God's a - gon - na build up Zi - on's
Great___ day! God's a gon - na build up Zi - on's
cresc. e accelerando
25
A Tempo
f
walls!
walls!
Zi - on's walls!
28

WE BELIEVE IN MUSIC

Composer: Kirby Shaw
Text: Kirby Shaw
Voicing: 2-Part

Cultural Context:
This energetic song inspires the singer to perform all types and styles of music, from Bach to rock, with great excitement and enthusiasm. Using scat syllables and a joyous text, this piece is a celebration of the music making experience.

Musical Terms:

sim. (simile) | **D.S. al Coda** | 𝄌 **CODA**

♩ = 160 | (staccato) | *melody*

Preparation:
Clap the rhythm of the opening phrase:

Once you are able to successfully clap the above rhythm, try the following:

- Chant the opening phrase. Remember that the syllable "du" should be performed in a legato or smooth style and the syllable "doot" should be performed in a short and staccato manner.
- As you continue to sing and repeat this opening phrase, listen as the teacher plays Part I. When Part I is able to sing its part, then Part II should listen as its part is played. When both parts are secure, answer the following questions:
  - Which voice part is singing the melody?
  - Which voice part is singing the supporting harmony?

Evaluation:
As you perform this piece, check that you are doing the following:

- When my part has the melody, it is clearly heard.
- When my part has the harmony line, it supports the melody line, but does not overpower it.
- During the opening phrase, I carefully sing all staccato and legato markings as written.

We Believe in Music

For 2-Part and Piano

Words and Music by KIRBY SHAW

* Use cue notes for fuller harmony

B
mf
Hel - lo, morn - in',
hel - lo, brand new day,
mak - in' mu - sic,
mak - in' good things come your way.
We're gon - na
ff

23
24
25
26
raise our voic - es high,
clear up to the sky,
gon - na
27
cresc.
28
29
30
Melody
feel fine!
Let our light shine!
We be - lieve in
Melody
cresc.
cresc.
C
f
32
33
mu - sic,
1. noth - ing can com - pare,
2. rock - in' to the beat,
f
f

we be - lieve in mu - sic,
1. let us take you there!
2. got to move these feet!
mp
f
Opt. hand claps
D
Du du doot du doot
du du doot, du du doot du du doot!
sim. through m. 45
Du du doot du doot

To Coda
end hand claps
44
45
46
du du doot, du du doot du du doot!
E
mf
48
49
50
Bach and Mo - zart, Folk and Fif - ties Gold,
mf
mp
f
mf
51
52
53
Mad - ri - gals and Spir - it - uals sung from the heart and soul.

54
55
56
— Gon - na sing out loud and strong — to
57
58
59
cresc.
last our whole life long, — mag - ic mel - o - dies, —
Melody
cresc.
D.S. al Coda (C)
60
61
62
Melody
— Mae - stro, if you please! — We be - lieve in
cresc.

CODA
64
65
We be-lieve in mu - sic.
We be-lieve in
66 cresc.
67
68 ff
mu - sic.
We be-lieve in mu - sic!
cresc.
ff
cresc.
ff
69
70
71
Du du doot du du doot!
8va

SONGS FOR SPECIAL TIMES

LAS MAÑANITAS (THE MORNING SONG)

Composer: Mexican Folk Song, arranged by Audrey Snyder
Text: Traditional Spanish, English Lyrics by Audrey Snyder
Voicing: 2-Part

Cultural Context:
"Las Mañanitas" is a traditional birthday song that is popular in Mexico as well as in many other Latin American countries. When this song is sung for young men or boys, the custom is to change the words "las muchachas bonitas" (the pretty girls) to "por ser hoy dia de tu santo" (because today is your holy patron's day). You may also replace the words "mi bien" with the name of the person being honored.

Musical Terms:

mf (mezzo forte)

mp (mezzo piano)

Preparation:
Practice pronouncing the Spanish text in "Las Mañanitas."

Spanish: *Estas son las mañanitas que cantaba el Rey David,*
Pronunciation: EH-stas sohn lahs ma-n(ee)ah-NEE-tahs keh kahn-TAH-bah ehl R̃AY dah-VEED

a las muchachas bonitas se las cantamos así:
a lahs moo-CHAH-chahs boh-NEE-tahs seh lahs kahn-TAH-mos ah-SEE

Despierta, mi bien, despierta, mira que ya amaneció,
deh-SP(EE)EHR̃-tah mee b(ee)ehn deh-SP(EE)EHR̃-tah MEE-r̃a keh yah ah-mah-neh-S(EE)OH

Ya los pajaritos cantan, la luna ya se metió,
yah lohs pa-ha-R̃EE-tohs KAHN-tahn, lah LOO-nah yah seh meh-(TEE)OH

Las mañanitas cantamos, las mañanitas cantamos.
lahs ma-n(ee)ah-NEE-tahs kahn-TAH-mohs

Evaluation:
Test yourself! See how well you can match the English word with the corresponding Spanish equivalent.

1. _____King David
2. _____pretty girls
3. _____we sing
4. _____wake up
5. _____look
6. _____little birds
7. _____has set, has gone

A. despierta
B. los pajaritos
C. mira
D. se metió
E. Rey David
F. muchachas bonitas
G. cantamos

Las Mañanitas

(The Morning Song)

For 2-Part and Piano

English Lyrics by AUDREY SNYDER

Mexican Folk Song
Arranged by AUDREY SNYDER

13
sí: Des - pier - ta, mi bien, des - pier - ta, mi - ra que ya_a-ma-ne-
G D7 G2 G Dsus D
12
Part I
ció, Ya los pa - ja-ri-tos can - tan, la lu-na ya se me -
Part II
ció, Ya los pa - ja-ri-tos can - tan, la lu-na ya se me -
G C G Am D
16
21
tió. Las ma-ña - ni - tas, las ma-ña - ni - tas can -
tió. Las ma-ña - ni - tas can - ta -
G D2sus Em D2sus
20

ta - mos, las ma-ña - ni - tas
can - ta -
mos,
las ma-ña - ni - tas can - ta -
G2 G
D2/F♯
G
D
24
mos.
Now we
mp
mf
mos. Now we sing las ma-ña - ni - tas as was
G2 G
G2
Am/G
28
31
sing las ma-ña - ni - tas as was sung so long a -
sung so long a - go, by King Dav - id to the
G2
Am/G
G2
31

mf
go, the sun - light's first glow. A -
mf
chil - dren to greet the sun - light's first glow. A -
Am/G G2 Am D G
34
wak - en, oh yes, a - wak - en and wel - come the ear - ly
wak - en, oh yes, a - wak - en and wel - come the ear - ly
D7 G2 G Dsus D
37
41
dawn, Now the birds are sweet - ly sing - ing, the sil - ver
mp
dawn, Loo loo loo
G C G
40

moon - light has gone. Las ma - ña - ni - tas,
loo loo loo loo, Las ma - ña -
mf
Am D G D2sus
43
las ma - ña - ni - tas, come join us, las ma - ña -
ni - tas, come join in the song,
Em D G2 G
46
ni - tas come join in the
las ma - ña - ni - tas, come join in the
D2/F♯ G D
49

53
mf
song. Es - tas son las ma - ña - ni - tas que can -
mp
song. La la la la la la la la
G2 G G2 Am/G
52
ta - ba el Rey Da - vid, a las mu - cha - chas bo -
la la la la la la la
G2 Am/G G2
55
mp
ni - tas se las can - ta - mos a - sí, can -
mf
la la la la la la la, Des -
Am/G G2 Am D G
58

61
ta - mos a -
pier - ta, mi bien, des - pier - ta, mi - ra que ya‿a - ma - ne -
D7 G2 G Dsus D
61
mf
sí, Ya los pa - ja - ri - tos can - tan, la lu - na ya se me -
mp
ció, La la la la la la la la la la
G C G Am D
64
69
tió. Las ma - ña - ni - tas, las ma - ña -
mf
la, Las ma - ña - ni - tas can -
G D2sus Em
68

ni - tas can - ta - mos, las ma - ña - ni - tas,
ta - mos, las ma - ña -
D2 D7 G2 G D2/F♯
71
come join in the
ni - tas, come join in the
G G2/D D2sus D7
74
rit.
song!
rit.
song!
G2
rit.
77

GOOD CHEER (FESTIVAL PROCESSION)

Composer: Based on a Medieval English Song, arranged by Audrey Snyder
Text: Audrey Snyder
Voicing: 2-Part any combination

Cultural Context:
This joyful piece is based on a two-part medieval song entitled "Edi Be Thu" which was written in the late 13th or early 14th century at the Priory of Llanthony in England. It is a wonderful piece to use for a madrigal dinner, a concert, or to perform when studying the traditions and customs of England during medieval times.

Audrey Snyder, the arranger of this piece, composes and arranges music with rare beauty, simplicity and charm. She is a highly regarded educator, clinician, and composer.

Musical Terms:

f (forte)

div. (divisi)

ff (fortissimo)

' (breath mark)

Preparation:
- Isolate and practice clapping or tapping the following rhythm before you sing the song.

- Can you find this rhythm pattern in your music? How many times does it occur?

Evaluation:
Select three students to step out in front of the choir and serve as "judges." They are to listen carefully as the choir performs "Good Cheer" mm. 19-26. The judges must determine if the choir was able to sing the rhythms correctly in this section. Repeat the process with new judges.

Good Cheer

(Festival Procession)

For 2-Part any combination with Hand Percussion and Optional Piano

Arranged by AUDREY SYNDER

Lyrics by AUDREY SNYDER
Based on a Medieval English Song

19
mer - ry hearts and spir - its bright. Sing we now most
glad some in - stru - ments then re - ply. Sing we now most
mer - ry hearts and spir - its bright. Sing we now most
glad - some in - stru - ments then re - ply. Sing we now most
17
joy - ful - ly, de - light - ing in your com - pa - ny,
joy - ful - ly, de - light - ing in your com - pa - ny,
joy - ful - ly, de - light - ing in your com - pa - ny,
joy - ful - ly, de - light - ing in your com - pa - ny,
20
Wel - come, wel - come from far and near, we wel - come you with
Wish - ing peace and good will to all who cel - e - brate with -
Wel - come, wel - come from far and near, we wel - come you with
Wish - ing peace and good will to all who cel - e - brate with -
23

1
all good cheer!
in this hall.
all good cheer!
in this hall.
f
26
2
36
mp
31
cresc.
ff
37

43
f
3. Wel - come, wel - come from far and near, we wel - come you with
f
3. Wel - come, wel - come from far and near, we wel - come you with
mf
43
all good cheer! Join with us on this fes - tive night with
all good cheer! Join with us on this fes - tive night with
46
51
mer - ry hearts and spir - its bright. Sing we now most joy - ful - ly, de -
mer - ry hearts and spir - its bright. Sing we now most joy - ful - ly, de -
mp
49

light - ing in your com - pa - ny, Wel - come, wel - come from
light - ing in your com - pa - ny, Wel - come, wel - come from
mf
53
far and near, we wel - come you with all good cheer, we
far and near, we wel - come you with all good cheer, we
56
ff
div.
cheer!
wel - come you with all good cheer, good cheer!
ff
wel - come you with all good cheer, good cheer!
f
59

Good Cheer

(Festival Procession)

PERCUSSION

Arranged by AUDREY SNYDER

FUM, FUM, FUM

Composer: Traditional Catalonian Carol, arranged by Audrey Snyder
Text: Traditional
Voicing: 2-Part (Opt. divisi)

Cultural Context:

"Fum, Fum, Fum" is a festive holiday carol that has its roots in a region called Catalonia, located in the Northeast corner of Spain. This light and lively folk melody, written in the minor mode, warmly celebrates the Christmas season. The syllables "fum, fum, fum," which have no specific meaning, punctuate each phrase. The optional tambourine part contributes to the joyous and spirited character of the music.

Musical Terms:

♩ = ca. 116	Unis. (unison)	div. (divisi)
cresc. (crescendo)	$\frac{2}{4}$	$\frac{3}{4}$
mf (mezzo forte)	***f*** (forte)	***ff*** (fortissimo)
mp (mezzo piano)	> (accent)	

Preparation:

Clap the rhythm of the opening phrase while tapping a steady quarter note pulse in your feet. Repeat this phrase until it is comfortable. Keep this crisp and snappy performing style in mind as you prepare to learn the pitches.

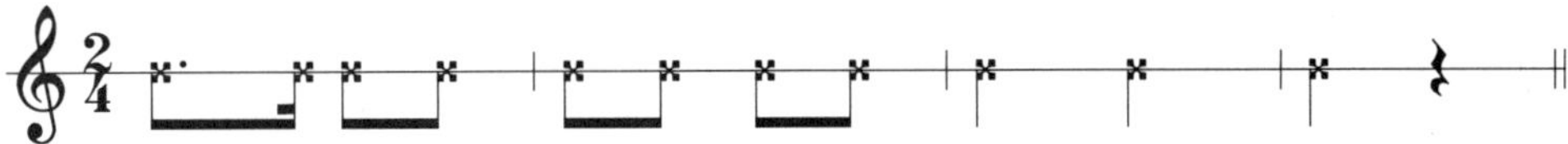

Evaluation:

- After you have learned this song very well, answer these questions:
  - Are you able to sing all the pitches and Spanish words clearly and correctly?
  - Are you able to recognize and sing the meter changes?
  - Can you correctly perform all the dynamic markings that are found in the score?
  - Can you sing this piece in a light, festive, and bouncy style?
- Keep working until you can do all of these things successfully.

Fum, Fum, Fum

For 2-Part (Opt. divisi) and Piano with Tambourine

Arranged by AUDREY SNYDER

Traditional Catalonian Carol

14
do ha por nues-tro a-mor el Ni-ño Dios, el Ni-ño Dios; Hoy de
Son of God is born on this love-ly Christ-mas morn. In a
14
la vir-gen Ma-ri-a en es-ta no-che tan fri-a, fum, fum, fum.
sta-ble dark and low-ly lies the in-fant King most ho-ly,
18
(shake)
23
mp
Re-go-ci-
The earth re-
mp
Can-ta vien a la cel-e-bra-ción, Can-ta
Sing with all good cheer, with all good cheer, Sing with
mp
continue sim.
23

Vein - ti cin - co de di - ciem - bre,
Sing with joy this Christ - mas sea - son,
31
f
ja - te, el mun - do cel - e - bra, Re - go - ci - ja - te,
joic - es, Come sing a joy - ful song, The earth re - joic - es,
mp
vien a la cel - e - bra - ción, Can - ta vien a la
all good cheer, with all good cheer, Sing with all good cheer,
mf
28
fum, fum, fum. Vein - ti cin - co de di - ciem - bre,
Sing with joy this Christ - mas sea - son,
el mun - do cel - e - bra, Re - go - ci - ja - te,
Come sing a joy - ful song, The earth re - joic - es,
cel - e - bra - ción, Can - ta vien a la
with all good cheer, Sing with all good cheer,
33

39
fum, fum, fum. Na - ci - do ha por nues - tro a mor el Ni - ño
For the Son of God is born on this
el mun - do cel - e - bra, Re - go - ci - ja - te,
Come sing a joy - ful song, The earth re - joic - es,
cel - e - bra - ción, Can - ta vien a la
with all good cheer, Sing with all good cheer,
Tacet
37

Dios, el Ni - ño Dios, Hoy de la Vir - gen Ma - ri - a
love - ly Christ - mas morn. In a sta - ble dark and low - ly
el mun - do cel - e - bra. en es -
Come sing a joy - ful song. lies the
cel - e - bra - ción, Hoy de la Vir - gen Ma - ri - a
with all good cheer. In a sta - ble dark and low - ly
41

48
ta no - che tan fri - a, fum, fum, fum. Fum, fum, fum,
in - fant King most ho - ly,
mf
(shake)
cresc.
div. ff
fum, fum, fum, fum, fum, fum!
ff
(shake)
f
(shake)

HANUKKAH, THE FESTIVAL OF LIGHTS

Composer: Jill Gallina
Text: Jill Gallina
Voicing: 2-Part

Cultural Context:

Hanukkah is an eight-day Jewish festival celebrating the rededication of the Temple after an attack by Antiochus of Syria in 165 BC. Hanukkah is also known as the Festival of Lights.

Musical Terms:

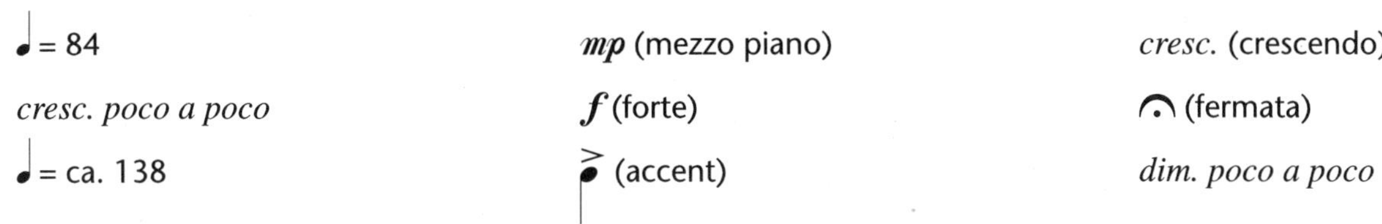

♩ = 84	*mp* (mezzo piano)	*cresc.* (crescendo)
cresc. poco a poco	*f* (forte)	(fermata)
♩ = ca. 138	(accent)	*dim. poco a poco*

Preparation:

"Hanukkah, Festival of Lights" includes the dotted quarter note/eighth note rhythmic pattern. Practice the following patterns. Make certain that each dotted quarter note is as long as three eighth notes.

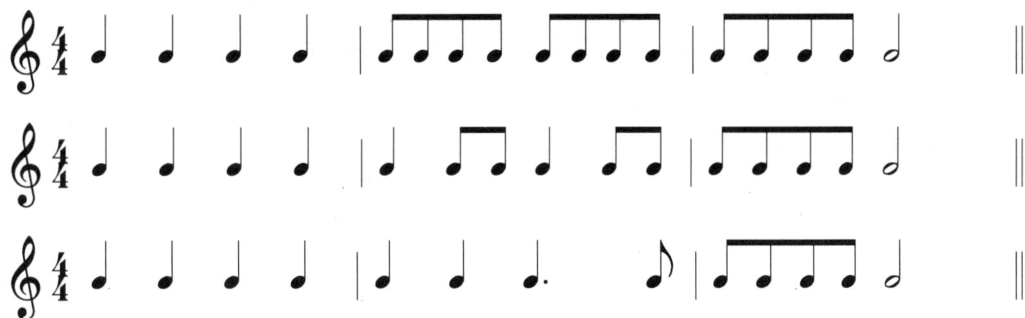

Evaluation:

After you can sing your part correctly, evaluate how well you can do the following:

- I can stay on my part securely while the other part is singing.
- I used different articulation in Section A (mm. 3-18) than I used in Section B (mm. 19-end).

Hanukkah, the Festival of Lights

For 2-Part and Piano

Words and Music by JILL GALLINA

mp
eight long days and nights to make this Fes - ti - val of Lights. Oh, we call
mp
eight long days and nights to make this Fes - ti - val of Lights. Oh, we call
8
11
Ha - nuk - kah the Fes - ti - val of Lights, and burn a can - dle for
Ha - nuk - kah the Fes - ti - val of Lights, and burn a can - dle for
mp
11
cresc. poco a poco
each of the eight nights. A time to dance and sing, so let the mu-sic play on this
cresc. poco a poco
each of the eight nights. A time to dance and sing, so let the mu-sic play on this
cresc. poco a poco
14

19 Faster (♩ = 138)
f
hap - py hol - i - day. Come now, let's turn, turn, turn.
hap - py hol - i - day. Come now, let's turn and turn and
17
We'll dance the hor - a and we'll turn and turn a - round._ And then we'll
turn, turn a - round. And then we'll
20
spin, spin, spin, just like a drei - dl to the sound.
spin and spin and spin to the
23

27
And now we'll dance, dance, dance.
sound. And now we'll dance and dance and
26
dim. poco a poco
We'll just keep danc - ing 'til the mu - sic fades a - way. As we
dim. poco a poco
dance, 'til the mu - sic fades a - way. As we
dim. poco a poco
28
cel - e - brate this hap - py hol - i - day.
cel - e - brate this hap - py hol - i - day.
31

35
f
Come now, let's turn, turn, turn. We'll dance the hor - a and we'll
f
Come now, let's turn and turn and turn,
f
34
turn and turn a - round._ And then we'll spin, spin, spin,
turn a - round. And then we'll spin and spin and
37
just like a drei - dl to the sound. And then we'll
spin to the sound._ And then we'll
40

43
dance, dance, dance. We'll just keep danc - ing 'til the
dance and dance and dance and dance, 'til the
43
mu - sic fades a - way.
As we cel - e - brate this
mu - sic fades a - way.
As we cel - e - brate this
45
hap - py hol - i - day.
Hey!
hap - py hol - i - day.
Hey!
48

SONGS FOR MIXED VOICES

DE COLORES (ALL THE COLORS)

Composer: Mexican Folk Song, arranged by John Leavitt
Text: Traditional Spanish
Voicing: 3-Part Mixed

Cultural Context:
"De Colores," a popular children's song, took on a new meaning in the early 1970's when it became a theme song for the Mexican-American civil rights movement. It was often sung at gatherings held by those who were striving for fair treatment for all people in the United States. Also, it is significant that the words refer to a world of many colors, which was felt to represent a world where all races and creeds would be treated equally.

Musical Terms:

$\frac{2}{2}$

cresc. (crescendo)

♩♩♩ (triplet)

p (piano)

mf (mezzo forte)

Preparation:
For better understanding, read the English translation of the Spanish words.

Oh, the colors! Oh the colors we see in the blossoming fields in the springtime.
All the colors, all the colors of bright feathered birds that return from a distance.
Oh, the colors! Oh, the colors that light up the sky in a beautiful rainbow!
And the colors of true love are brightest, and these are the colors I love most of all.
And the colors of true love are brightest, and these are the colors I love most of all.

Evaluation:
Discuss images found in this song. The image of color is represented through flowers, birds, a rainbow, and true love. What is the overall theme of this song? Why do you feel some Mexican-Americans used this song to express their feelings during their struggle for equal rights?

De Colores
(All the Colors)

For 3-Part Mixed and Piano

Arranged by JOHN LEAVITT

Mexican Folk Song

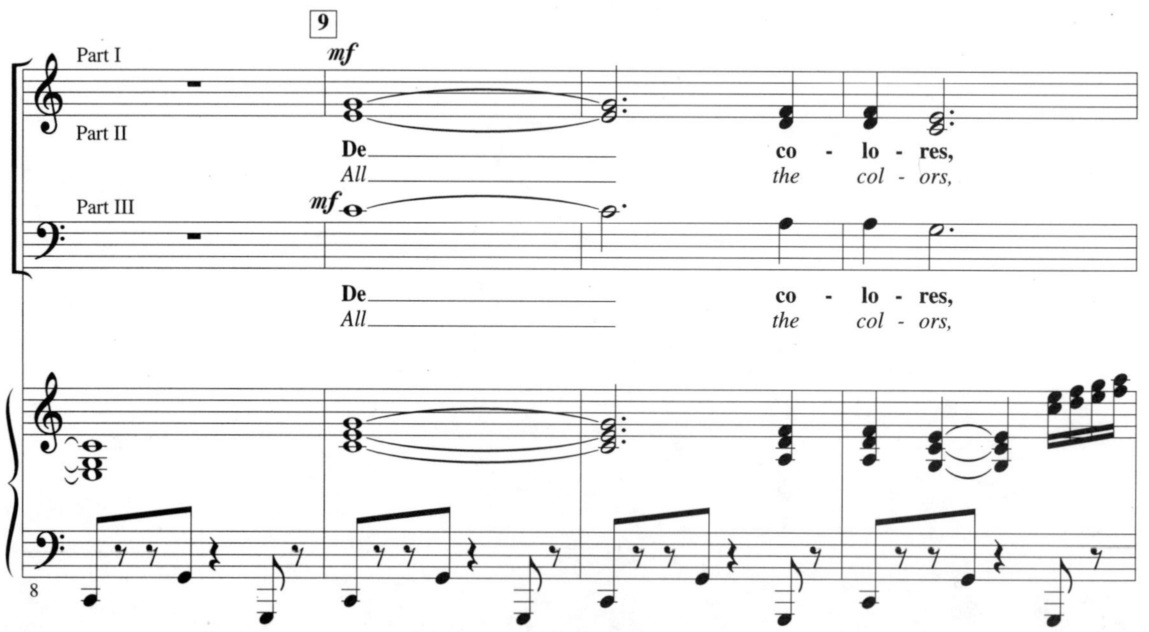

de co - lo - res se vis - ten los cam - pos en la pri - ma -
all the col - ors that bloom in the mead - ows are col - ors of
de co - lo - res se vis - ten los cam - pos en la pri - ma -
all the col - ors that bloom in the mead - ows are col - ors of
12
17
Unis.
ve - ra. De co -
spring - time. All the
ve - ra. De co -
spring - time. All the
15
lo - res, de co - lo - res son los pa - ja -
col - ors, all the col - ors that dance in the
lo - res, de co - lo - res son los pa - ja -
col - ors, all the col - ors that dance in the
19

3
ri - tos que vie - nen de a - fue - ra.
sky are the col - ors of rain - bows.
ri - tos que vie - nen de a - fue - ra.
sky are the col - ors of rain - bows.
22
25
De co - lo - res,
All the col - ors,
De co - lo - res,
All the col - ors,
25
de co - lo - res es el ar - co i - ris que ve - mos lu -
all the col - ors of na - ture spring forth to make my heart
de co - lo - res es el ar - co i - ris que ve - mos lu -
all the col - ors of na - ture spring forth to make my heart
28

33
Unis. p cresc.
cir, y por e - so los gran-des a -
sing. Then I know why the col - ors of
p cresc.
cir, y por e - so los gran-des a -
sing. Then I know why the col - ors of
p cresc.
31
mo - res de mu-chos co - lo - res me gus - tan a mi,
spring-time are bring-ing me joy and a heart_ full of love,
Unis. mf
los a -
Yes I
mf
mf
34
mo - res de mu-chos co - lo - res me gus-tan a mi.
know why the col - ors of spring-time are bring-ing me joy.
37

(𝅗𝅥 = ♩.)
(𝅗𝅥 = ♩.)
40
43
De ___ co - lo - res, ___
All ___ the col - ors, ___
De ___ co - lo - res, ___
All ___ the col - ors, ___
43
de co - lo - res se vis - ten los cam - pos en la pri - ma -
all the col - ors that bloom in the mead-ows are col - ors of
de co - lo - res se vis - ten los cam - pos en la pri - ma -
all the col - ors that bloom in the mead-ows are col - ors of
46

51
ve - ra.
spring - time.
De
All
ve - ra.
spring - time.
De
All
49
Unis.
co - lo - res,
the col - ors,
de co -
All the
co - lo - res,
the col - ors,
de co -
All the
52
lo - res son los pa - ja - ri - tos que vie - nen de a - fue - ra.
col - ors that dance in the sky are the col - ors of rain - bows.
lo - res son los pa - ja - ri - tos que vie - nen de a - fue - ra.
col - ors that dance in the sky are the col - ors of rain - bows.
55

59
(♩. = 𝅗𝅥)
De co - lo - res,
All the col - ors,
de co - lo - res es el - ar - co
all the col - ors of na - ture spring
i - ris que ve - mos lu - cir,
forth to make my heart sing.
Unis. p cresc.
y por
Then I
58
61
64

67
e - so los gran-des a - mo - res de mu - chos co - lo - res me gus - tan a
know why the col - ors of spring-time are bring - ing me joy and a heart_ full of
e - so los gran-des a - mo - res de mu - chos co - lo - res me gus - tan a
know why the col - ors of spring-time are bring - ing me joy and a heart_ full of
67
mf cresc.
mi, los a - mo - res de mu - chos co - lo - res me gus - tan a
love, Then I know why the col - ors of spring-time are bring - ing me
mf cresc.
mi, los a - mo - res de mu - chos co - lo - res me gus - tan a
love, Then I know why the col - ors of spring-time are bring - ing me
mf cresc.
70
mi.
joy!
clap
div.
clap
mi.
joy!
8va
8vb
73

TINGA LAYO

Composer: West Indies Folk Song, arranged by Cristi Cary Miller
Text: Traditional
Voicing: 3-Part Mixed

Cultural Context:

Calypso is a very popular type of song in the Caribbean islands, especially in Trinidad, where this art form was developed. Calypso has a long history that was influenced by African slave songs. Modern forms of calypso contain text that may be silly, serious, or humorous, and describes news, world events, or village happenings. The melodies, as well as the accompaniments played by brass, percussion, or steel drums, have syncopated dance-like rhythms.

Musical Terms:

mp (mezzo piano)	*cresc.* (crescendo)	*f* (forte)
sub. f (subito forte)	*mf* (mezzo forte)	syncopation
calypso		

Preparation:

Syncopation is a rhythmic pattern that stresses notes on the "offbeat." Practice the syncopated patterns below and then try to find these patterns in your music.

Evaluation:

To check that you can perform the syncopated rhythms correctly, play a game "Who Can Guess the Rhythm?" Select a student to clap or tap one of the three rhythm patterns found in the Preparation section of this lesson. The rest of the class must guess which rhythm pattern the student was clapping. Continue the game until everyone has had a chance to clap or tap a rhythm.

Tinga Layo

For 3-Part Mixed and Piano with Optional Percussion

Arranged by CRISTI CARY MILLER

West Indies Folk Song

*Pronounced "ting-ah lay-oh"

Run, lit - tle don - key, run. Tin - ga, Tin - ga
Run, lit - tle don - key, run. Tin - ga lay -
Run, lit - tle don - key, run. Oh, Tin - ga
7
lay - o! Run, lit - tle don - key, run.
o! Run, lit - tle don - key, run. Me don - key
Me don - key
lay - o! Run, lit - tle don - key, run.
f
f
10

13
f
Oh, Tin - ga lay - o! Tin-ga lay - o, lay -
eat, me don - key sleep, me don - key kick wid him two hind
walk, me don - key talk, me don - key eat wid a spoon and
f
Tin-ga lay - o! Me don - key sleep. Oh, Tin-ga lay - o, lay -
13
13
mf
o! Oh, Tin - ga lay - o!
mf
feet. Me don - key eat, me don - key sleep, me don - key
fork. Me don - key walk, me don - key talk, me don - key
mf
o! Tin-ga lay - o, me don - key sleep. Oh,
mf
16

21
mp
Tin-ga lay-o, lay - o! Tin-ga, Tin-ga
kick wid him two hind feet.
eat wid a spoon and fork.
Tin - ga lay -
Tin-ga lay-o, lay - o! Oh, Tin - ga
21
19
lay - o!
o!
lay - o!
Run, lit - tle don - key, run!
Run, lit - tle don - key, run!
Run, lit - tle don - key, run!
22

1
2
29
Tin - ga
f
Tin - ga, — Tin-ga
1
2
29
f
26
mp
Run, lit - tle don - key, run, me don - key.
mp
Run, lit - tle don - key, run, me don - key.
lay - o! —
mp
30

mp
Run, lit - tle don - key,
mp
Run, lit - tle don - key,
f
Oh, Tin - ga lay - o!
f
mp
33
cresc.
run! Tin-ga lay - o! f Tin - ga
cresc.
run! Tin-ga lay - o!
cresc.
Run, lit - tle don - key,
cresc.
36

39
lay - o! Run, lit - tle don - key,
f
Tin - ga lay -
f
run! Tin - ga lay -
39
f
39
run. Tin - ga lay - o!
o! Tin - ga
o! Don - key, run! Tin - ga
42

47
Run, lit - tle don - key, run. Me don - key eat, me don - key
lay - o! Tin-ga lay - o!
lay - o! Tin-ga lay - o!
47
45
sleep, me don - key kick wid him two hind feet. Tin - ga
Tin-ga lay - o! Tin-ga lay - o, lay - o!
Tin-ga lay - o! Tin-ga lay - o, lay - o! Don - key,
48

lay - o! Run, lit - tle don - key,
Tin - ga lay -
run! Tin - ga lay -
51
sub. f
run! Run, lit - tle don - key, run!
o! Run, lit - tle don - key, run!
o! Run, lit - tle don - key, run!
mp
54

THIS LITTLE LIGHT OF MINE

Composer: Traditional, arranged by Neil A. Johnson
Text: Traditional
Voicing: 3-Part Mixed

Cultural Context:

Neil A. Johnson has arranged "This Little Light of Mine" using stylistic features associated with gospel music. Pairs of eighth notes, for example, should "swing," such that the first eighth note is held longer than the second eighth note is held. Thus, when singing the two eighth notes on the word "little," the first syllable takes more than half of a quarter note, while the second syllable takes less than half.

Musical Terms:

♩ = 76	♫ = ♩ ♪ (triplet 3) (swing)	*f* (forte)
mp (mezzo piano)	*mf* (mezzo forte)	𝅗𝅥 = 84
rit. (ritardando)	N.B. (no breath)	*a tempo*
(tenuto)	(accent)	gospel music

Preparation:

Practice the following 3-part chord patterns a cappella as a warm-up before rehearsing "This Little Light of Mine."

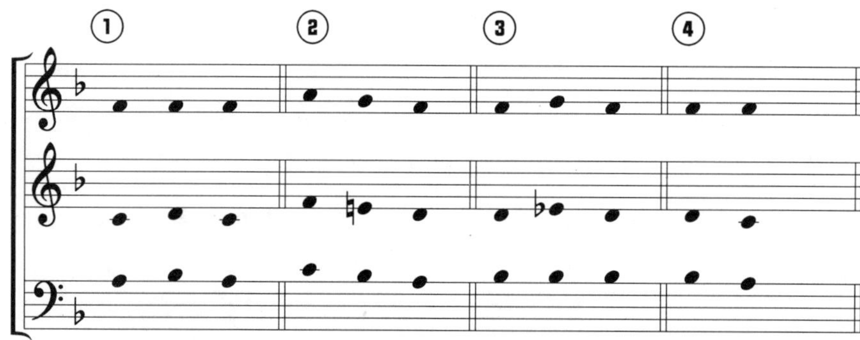

Evaluation:

- In groups of 6 or 9 singers, perform the above patterns for a group of others listening. Answer these questions about the groups' performance.
  - Was each chord balanced, that is, are all three pitches in each chord at the same volume?
  - Was one part too loud or too soft?
  - Were the chords in tune?
  - Were the singers shaping the vowels uniformly?
- Take turns singing and listening. Sing with different groups of people.

This Little Light of Mine

For 3-Part Mixed and Piano

Traditional
Arranged by NEIL A. JOHNSON

11
mf
mine, I'm gon-na let it shine. This lit-tle light of
mine, I'm gon-na let it shine. This lit-tle light of
mine, I'm gon-na let it shine. This lit-tle light of
8
rit. N.B. a tempo
mine, I'm gon-na let it shine ev-'ry day, ev-'ry
mine, I'm gon-na let it shine ev-'ry day, ev-'ry
mine, I'm gon-na let it shine ev-'ry day, ev-'ry
12

rit.
Much faster (𝅗𝅥 = 84 in two)
day, I'm gon - na let my lit - tle light shine.
rit.
day, I'm gon - na let my lit - tle light shine.
rit.
day, I'm gon - na let my lit - tle light shine.
Much faster (𝅗𝅥 = 84 in two)
rit.
mf
16
Ped.
19
mf
This lit - tle light of mine, I'm gon - na let it shine.
mf
This lit - tle light of mine, I'm gon - na let it shine.
mf
This lit - tle light of mine, I'm gon - na let it shine.
19
19

This lit-tle light of mine,
I'm gon-na let it shine.
This lit-tle light of mine,
I'm gon-na let it shine.
This lit-tle light of mine,
I'm gon-na let it shine.
23
27
mf
N.B.
This lit-tle light of mine,
I'm gon-na let it shine ev-'ry
mf
N.B.
This lit-tle light of mine,
I'm gon-na let it shine ev-'ry
N.B.
mf
This lit-tle light of mine,
I'm gon-na let it shine ev-'ry
27
mf
27

day, ev - 'ry day, I'm gon - na let my lit - tle light shine. On a
day, ev - 'ry day, I'm gon - na let my lit - tle light shine. On a
day, ev - 'ry day, I'm gon - na let my lit - tle light shine. On a
31
35
mf
Solo
All
Solo
All
Mon - day He gave the gift of love, on Tues - day peace came from a - bove, on
mf
Mon - day on Tues - day on
mf
Mon - day on Tues - day on
35
mf
35

Solo
All
Solo
Wednes - day told me to have more faith, on Thurs - day gave me just a
Wednes - day on Thurs - day
Wednes - day on Thurs - day
39
43
All
Solo
All
lit - tle more grace, on Fri - day told me to watch and pray, on
on Fri - day on
on Fri - day on
43
42

Solo
All
cresc.
Sat - ur - day told me just what to say, on Sun - day gave me the
cresc.
Sat - ur - day on Sun - day gave me the
cresc.
Sat - ur - day on Sun - day gave me the
cresc.
45
f
pow'r di - vine just to let my lit - tle light shine.
f
pow'r di - vine just to let my lit - tle light shine.
f
pow'r di - vine just to let my lit - tle light shine.
f
48

51
mf
This lit - tle light of mine,
I'm gon - na let it shine.
mf
This lit - tle light of mine,
I'm gon - na let it shine.
mf
This lit - tle light of mine,
I'm gon - na let it shine.
51
mf
51
This lit - tle light of mine,
I'm gon - na let it shine.
This lit - tle light of mine,
I'm gon - na let it shine.
This lit - tle light of mine,
I'm gon - na let it shine.
55

59
N.B.
This lit - tle light of mine, I'm gon - na let it shine ev - 'ry
This lit - tle light of mine, I'm gon - na let it shine ev - 'ry
This lit - tle light of mine, I'm gon - na let it shine ev - 'ry
day, ev - 'ry day, I'm gon - na let my lit - tle light shine. On a
day, ev - 'ry day, I'm gon - na let my lit - tle light shine. On a
day, ev - 'ry day, I'm gon - na let my lit - tle light shine. On a
63

2

68

f *

shine. ___ This lit - tle light of mine, ___

f *

shine. This lit - tle light of mine, ___

f *

shine. This lit - tle light of mine, ___

2

68

f

67

I'm gon-na let it shine. ___ This lit-tle light of mine, ___

I'm gon-na let it shine. ___ This lit-tle light of mine, ___

I'm gon-na let it shine. ___ This lit-tle light of mine, ___

* *Some boys' voices may double soprano melody.*

76
I'm gon-na let it shine. This lit-tle light of mine,
I'm gon-na let it shine. This lit-tle light of mine,
I'm gon-na let it shine. This lit-tle light of mine,
76
74
I'm gon-na let it shine ev-'ry day, ev - 'ry day, ev - 'ry
I'm gon-na let it shine ev-'ry day, ev - 'ry day, ev - 'ry
I'm gon-na let it shine ev-'ry day, ev - 'ry day, ev - 'ry
78

day, ev - 'ry day, I'm gon - na let my lit - tle light
day, ev - 'ry day, I'm gon - na let my lit - tle light
day, ev - 'ry day, I'm gon - na let my lit - tle light
82
shine.
shine.
shine.
(opt. 8va)
86

GLOSSARY

a cappella [It.] (ah-kah-PEH-lah) - Singing without instrumental accompaniment.

accelerando (*accel.*) [It.] (ahk-chel-leh-RAHN-doh) - Becoming faster; a gradual increase in tempo.

accent (>) - Stress or emphasize a note (or chord) over others around it. Accents occur by singing the note louder or stressing the beginning consonant or vowel.

accidentals - Symbols that move the pitch up or down a half step.

- sharp (♯) - raises the pitch one half step.
- flat (♭) - lowers the pitch one half step.
- natural (♮) - cancels a previous *sharp* or *flat*. (When it cancels a flat, the pitch is raised one half step; when it cancels a sharp, the pitch is lowered one half step).

Accidentals affect all notes of the same pitch that follow the accidental within the same measure, or if an altered note is *tied* over a *barline*.

adagio [It.] (ah-DAH-jee-oh) - Tempo marking indicating slow.

agitato [It.] (ah-jee-TAH-toh) - Agitated.

al fine [It.] (ahl FEE-neh) - To ending. An indicator following *D.C.* or *D.S.*. From the Latin *finis,* "to finish."

alla breve [It.] (ahl-lah BREH-veh) - A duple time signature, usually $\frac{2}{2}$.

allargando (*allarg.*) [It.] (ahl-lahr-GAHN-doh) - Broadening, becoming slower, sometimes with an accompanying *crescendo.*

allegretto [It.] (ah-leh-GREH-toh) - Slightly slower than *allegro.*

allegro [It.] (ah-LEH-groh) - Tempo marking indicating fast.

alto - A treble voice that is lower than the *soprano,* usually written in the *treble clef.*

andante [It.] (ahn-DAHN-teh) - Tempo marking indicating medium or "walking" tempo.

arranger - The person who takes an already existing composition and reorganizes it to fit a new instrumentation or voicing.

art song - A serious vocal composition, generally for solo voice and piano.

articulation - The clear pronunciation of text using the lips, teeth, and tongue. The singer must attack consonants crisply and use proper vowel formation.

a tempo - Return to the original tempo.

ballad - A narrative song dealing with dramatic episodes; a simpler, sentimental song; an air. Many ballads have been passed down orally for generations.

bar - See *measure.*

barline - A vertical line that divides the staff into smaller sections called measures. A double barline indicates the end of a section or piece of music.

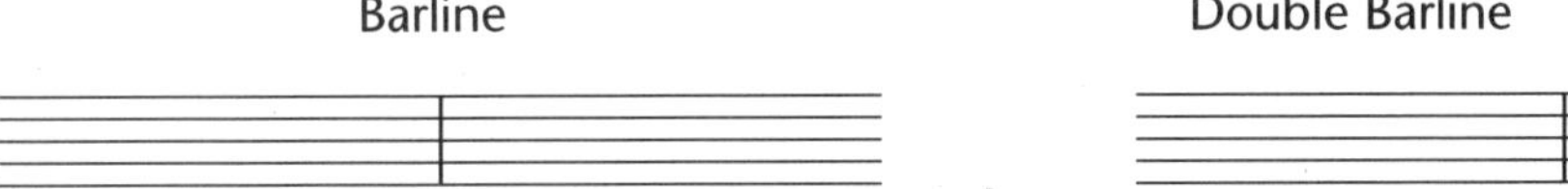

Baroque Period (ca. 1600-1750) - (bah-ROHK) The period in Western music history that extended from 1600 to about 1750; also the musical styles of that period. The style features of most Baroque music include frequent use of *polyphony*; fast, motor-like rhythms; and use of the *chorale*. Some famous Baroque composers were Johann Sebastian Bach, George Frideric Handel, and Antonio Vivaldi.

bass - A male voice written in *bass clef* that is lower than a *tenor* voice.

bass clef - The symbol at the beginning of the staff used for lower voices and instruments, and the piano left hand. It generally refers to pitches lower than *middle* C. The two dots are on either side of F, so it is often referred to as the F clef.

beat - The unit of recurring pulse in music.

blue notes - Notes found in the *blues* scale which give it a unique sound. They are the flatted third and flatted seventh *scale* degrees of the *major* scale. Authentic blue notes are not exactly a flatted third or seventh, but fall somewhere in between the regular third (or seventh) and the flatted third (or seventh). See also *blues.*

blues - One of America's unique contributions to Western music. The blues is a style of music that has origins in early twentieth century African-American cultures. It combines elements of *syncopation, blue notes,* and many elements found in *spirituals* of the early American slaves. See also *blue notes.*

breath mark (,) - An indicator within a phrase or melody where the musician should breathe. See also *no breath* and *phrase marking.*

call and response - Alternation between two performers or groups of performers. Often used in *spirituals*, this technique begins with a leader (or group) singing a phrase followed by a response of the same phrase (or continuation of the phrase) by a second group.

calypso - A rhythm and song style, originally from Trinidad, that often contains satirical lyrics.

canon - A musical form in which a melody in one part is followed a short time later by other parts performing the same melody. Canons are sometimes called *rounds.*

cantata [It.] (cahn-TAH-tah) - A large work (originally sacred) involving solos, chorus, organ, and occasionally orchestra. The cantata tells a story through text and music. Johann Sebastian Bach wrote a cantata for each Sunday of the church year.

carol - A song of English origin dating back to the Middle Ages with subject matter pertaining to the Virgin Mary or Christmas. Christmas carols often were usually *strophic* in nature often with a recurring refrain between verses. Similar songs existed in other cultures—*noël* in France and *Weinachtslied* in Germany—although today all of these Christmas songs are referred to as carols.

chantey - A song sung by sailors in rhythm with their work.

chord - Three or more pitches sounding at the same time or in succession as in a broken chord. See also *interval.*

chorus - 1. A group of singers of secular music. 2. The *refrain* of a song.

chromatic - Moving up or down by half steps, often outside of the key. Also the name of a *scale* composed entirely of half steps (all twelve pitches within an *octave*). The chromatic scale is distinct from the *diatonic* scale.

Classical Period (ca. 1750-1835) - The period in Western music history beginning in Italy in 1750 and continuing until about 1825. Music of the Classical Period emphasized balance of phrase and structure. Ludwig von Beethoven, Wolfgang Amadeus Mozart, and Joseph Haydn were famous composers from the Classical Period.

clef - The symbol at the beginning of the staff that identifies a set of pitches. See also *bass clef* and *treble clef.*

coda (𝄌) [It.] (COH-dah) - Ending. A concluding portion of a composition.

common time (𝄴) - Another name for the meter $\frac{4}{4}$. See also *cut time.*

composer - The writer or creator of a song or musical composition. See also *arranger.*

compound meter - Meters which have a multiple of 3 such as 6 or 9 (but not 3 itself). Compound meter reflects the note that receives the division unlike *simple meter.* (Ex. $\frac{6}{8}$ = six divisions to the beat in two groups of three where the eighth note receives one division.) An exception to the compound meter rule is when the music occurs at a slow tempo, then the music is felt in beats rather than divisions. See also *meter* and *time signature.*

con [It.] (kohn) - With.

counterpoint - The combination of two or more melodic lines. Counterpoint is the the core element of *polyphony.*

crescendo (*cresc.* or <) [It.] (kreh-SHEN-doh) - Gradually growing louder. The opposite of *decrescendo.*

cued notes - Smaller notes indicating either *optional harmony* or notes from another voice part.

cut time (𝄵) - $\frac{2}{2}$ time, the half note gets the beat.

da capo (D.C.) [It.] (dah KAH-poh) - Repeat from the beginning. See also *dal segno* and *al fine.*

dal segno (D.S.) [It.] (dahl SEHN-yoh) - Go back to the sign (𝄋) and repeat.

D.C. al fine [It.] - Repeat from the beginning to *fine* or end. See also *da capo* and *al fine.*

decrescendo (*decresc.* or >) [It.] (deh-kreh-SHEN-doh) - Gradually growing softer. The opposite of *crescendo.* See also *diminuendo.*

descant - A high ornamental voice part often lying above the melody.

diatonic - Step by step movement within a regular *scale* (any key). A combination of the seven whole and half steps (of different pitch names) within a key. Distinct from *chromatic.*

diminuendo (*dim.*) [It.] (dih-min-new-EN-doh) - Gradually growing softer. See also *decrescendo.*

diphthong (DIF-thong) - A combination of two vowel sounds consisting of a primary vowel sound and a secondary vowel sound. The secondary vowel sound is (usually) at the very end of the diphthong. (Ex. The word "I" is really a diphthong using an "ah" and an "ee." The "ee" is a very brief sound at the end of the word.)

dissonance - A dissonant interval is any interval that is not contained in a major (or minor) triad like a second, seventh, diminished fifth, etc. A dissonant chord is one that contains at least one dissonant interval.

divisi (div.) [It.] (dee-VEE-see) - Divide; the parts divide.

dolce [It.] (DOHL-cheh) - Sweetly; usually soft as well.

dominant chord (abbreviated V) - The name of the triad built on the fifth degree of the major scale. Dominant is also a category of harmony that evokes a feeling of momentum.

downbeat - The accented first beat of the measure.

drone/bourdon - 1. Any instrument that plays only a constant pitch or pitches. 2. A long, sustained tone in a piece of music, often intended to imitate the sound of a drone.

D.S. al Coda [It.] (ahl KOH-dah) - Repeat from the sign (𝄋) and sing the *coda* when you see the symbol (𝄌).

D.S. al fine [It.] (ahl FEE-neh) - Repeat from the sign (𝄋) to *fine* or ending.

duple - Any *time signature* or group of beats that is a multiple of 2.

dynamic - The loudness or softness of a line of music. Dynamic changes may occur frequently within a composition.

endings - |1. |2. (First and second endings) Alternate endings to a repeated section.

enharmonic - Identical tones which are named and written differently. For instance, F♯ and G♭ are the same note, they are "enharmonic" with each other.

ensemble - A group of musicians (instrumentalists, singers, or some combination) who perform together.

fermata (𝄐) [It.] (fur-MAH-tah) - Hold the indicated note (or rest) for longer than its value; the length is left up to the interpretation of the director or the performer.

fine [It.] (FEE-neh) - Ending. From the Latin *finis,* "to finish."

flat (♭) - An *accidental* that lowers the pitch of a note one half step. Flat also refers to faulty intonation when the notes are sung or played sightly under the correct pitch.

folk song - Songs passed down through oral tradition. Traditional music that reflects a locale or a national feeling.

form - The design and structure of a composition or section of a composition.

forte (*f*) [It.] (FOR-teh) - Loud.

fortissimo (*ff*) [It.] (for-TEE-see-moh) - Very loud.

freely - A style marking permitting liberties with tempo, dynamics, and style. *Rubato* may also be incorporated.

gospel music - 1. Anglo-American Protestant evangelical hymns usually with simple, *strophic* melodies set *homophonically* to strong tonal progressions. 2. Black American Protestant sacred singing where the vocalists improvise simple melodies by singing in full and/or falsetto voice, by adding *melismas* and *syncopation,* by adding *blue notes,* by freely extending or repeating any fragment of the text.

grand staff - A grouping of two staves.

half step - The smallest distance (or *interval*) between two notes on a keyboard. Shown symbolically (**v**). The *chromatic* scale is composed entirely of half steps.

half time - See *cut time.*

harmonic interval - *Intervals* played simultaneously.

harmonic minor - The minor scale in which the 7th degree of the scale is raised a half step to create a strong harmonic push toward the tonic. The awkward interval of 3 half steps between the 6th and 7th scale tones makes this scale pattern difficult to sing.

harmony - Two or more musical tones sounding simultaneously.

head voice - The upper register of the voice.

homophonic - See homophony.

homophony [Gr.] (haw-MAW-faw-nee) - Music in which melodic interest is concentrated in one voice part and may have subordinate accompaniment (distinct from *polyphony* in which all voice parts are equal). Homophony is also music which consists of two or more voice parts with similar or identical rhythms. From the Greek words meaning "same sounds," homophony could be described as being "hymn-style."

hushed - A style marking indicating a soft, whispered tone.

imitation - The successive statement of a melody, theme, or motive by two or more parts.

interval - The distance between two pitches.

intonation - Accuracy of pitch.

key - The organization of tonality around a single pitch (*key-note*). See also *key-note* and *key signature.*

key-note - The pitch which is the tonal center of a key. The first tone (note) of a scale. It is also called the *tonic.* A key is named after the key-note; for example in the key of A♭, A♭ is the key-note. See also *key* and *key signature.*

key signature - The group of *sharps* or *flats* at the beginning of a staff which combine to indicate the locations of the key-note and configuration of the *scale.* If there are no sharps or flats, the key is automatically C major or A minor.

B♭ major or G minor

larghetto [It.] (lahr-GHEH-toh) - Slightly slower than *largo.*

ledger lines (or leger lines) - The short lines used to extend the lines and spaces of the *staff.*

leading tone chord (abbreviated vii°) - The tone and chord (triad built on the seventh degree) in the major scale which has the strongest (and shortest) progression toward the tonic.

legato [It.] (leh-GAH-toh) - Smooth and connected. Opposite of *staccato.*

lento [It.] (LEHN-toh) - Slow.

lied [Ger. pl. Lieder] (leet; LEE-dehr) - In German, a musical term applying to any song. By the middle 1800s the lied developed into what has later been termed the artsong–a composition in which composers combined poetry and voice with piano accompaniment to create a new musical expression. See also chanson and *madrigal.*

lift (/) - An indication within a musical line for a brief stop in motion or momentum. Lifts are used between phrases or to set off important notes or words.

madrigal - A kind of 16th century Italian composition based on secular poetry. Madrigals were popular into the 17th century.

maestoso [It.] (mah(ee)-STOH-soh) - Majestic.

major key/scale/mode - A specific arrangement of whole steps and half steps in the following order:

Letter Names:	G	A	B	C	D	E	F♯	G
Moveable Do:	do	re	mi	fa	sol	la	ti	do
Fixed Do:	sol	la	ti	do	re	mi	fi	sol
Numbers:	1	2	3	4	5	6	7	1

See also *minor key/scale/mode.*

marcato [It.] (mahr-KAH-toh) - Marked or stressed, march-like.

mass - The central religious service of the Roman Catholic Church. It consists of several sections divided into two groups: Proper of the Mass (text changes for every day) and Ordinary of the Mass (text stays the same in every mass). Between the years 1400 and 1600 the mass assumed its present form consisting of the Kyrie, Gloria, Credo, Sanctus, and Agnus Dei. It may include chants, hymns, and psalms as well. The mass also developed into large musical works for chorus, soloists, and even orchestra.

measure - A group of beats divided by *barlines.* Measures are sometimes called *bars.* The first beat of each measure is usually accented.

melisma - Long groups of notes sung on one syllable of text.

melodic interval - Notes that comprise an *interval* played in succession.

melodic minor - The minor scale in which the 6th and 7th degrees of the scale are raised a half step when ascended and lowered to their original *natural minor* positions when descending.

melody - A succession of musical tones; also the predominant line in a song.

meno mosso [It.] (MEH-noh MOH-soh) - From the Italian *meno* (less) and *mosso* (moved). *Meno mosso* means less motion, or slower.

meter - A form of rhythmic organization (grouping of beats). The kind of meter designated by the *time signature.* See also *simple* and *compound meters.*

meter signature - See *time signature.*

metronome marking - A marking which appears over the top staff of music which indicates the kind of note which will get the beat, and the number of beats per minute as measured by a metronome. It reveals the *tempo.* (Ex. (♩= 100)).

mezzo forte (*mf* **)** [It.] (MEH-tsoh FOR-teh) - Medium loud.

mezzo piano (*mp* **)** [It.] (MEH-tsoh pee-AH-noh) - Medium soft.

middle C - The C which is located closest to the middle of the piano keyboard. Middle C can be written in either the *treble* or *bass clef.*

minor key/scale/mode - A specific arrangement of whole steps and half steps in the following order:

Letter Names:	D	E	F	G	A	B♭	C	D
Moveable La:	la	ti	do	re	mi	fa	sol	la
Fixed La:	re	mi	fa	sol	la	te	do	re
Numbers:	1	2	3	4	5	6	7	1

See also *major key/scale/mode.*

mixed meter - Frequently changing meters or *time signatures* within a piece of music.

Mixolydian (mix-oh-LID-ee-an) - A medieval mode starting on the fifth degree of the *diatonic* scale.

modal - Characterized by the use of *modes*, especially the church modes of the Middles Ages and Renaissance.

mode - An earlier system of pitch organization often referred to as *church modes.* These were different arrangements of whole and half steps within an octave and were used in early music, including the *chant.* The commonly used modes in early music are: Ionian, Dorian, Phrygian, Lydian, Mixolydian, Aeolian.

moderato [It.] (mah-deh-RAH-toh) - Moderate tempo.

modulation - Changing keys within a song. Adjust to the *key signature*, the *key-note*, and proceed.

molto [It.] (MOHL-toh) - Much, very. (Ex. molto rit. = greatly slowing)

monophonic - See monophony.

monophony - Music which consists of a single melody. This earliest form of composition is from the Greek words meaning "one sound." Chant or *plainsong* is monophony.

motet (moh-teht) - A major type of musical composition from the 1200s into the 1700s. The motet went through many different forms and developments beginning with the simpler medieval motet and progressing to the more intricate *Renaissance* motet which is generally considered a *polyphonic* setting of sacred Latin text.

moto [It.] (moh-toh) - Motion.

mysterioso [It.] (mih-steer-ee-OH-soh) - A style marking indicating a mysterious or haunting mood.

natural (♮) - Cancels a previous *sharp* (♯) or *flat* (♭). (When it cancels a flat, the pitch is raised one half step; when it cancels a sharp, the pitch is lowered one half step.)

natural minor - See *minor key/scale/mode.*

no breath (♪ ♪ or N.B.**)** - An indication by either the *composer/arranger* or the editor of where *not* to breathe in a line of music. See also *phrase marking.*

non [It.] (nohn) - Not.

notation - All written notes and symbols which are used to represent music.

octave - The *interval* between two notes of the same name. Octaves can be indicated within a score using *8va* (octave above) and *8vb* (octave below).

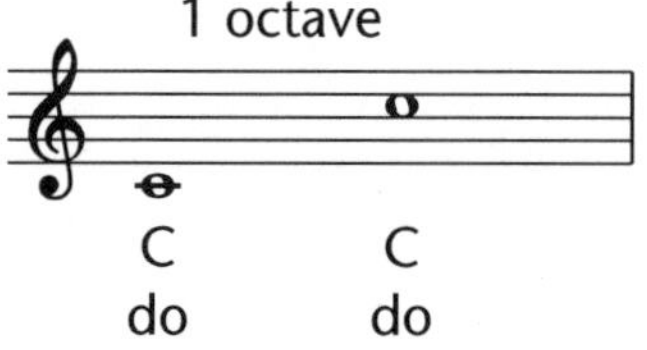

oratorio - a longer choral composition of religious or contemplative nature usually performed in a concert hall or church by solo voices, chorus, and orchestra. An oratorio is longer and has a more narrative libretto than a sacred cantata.

ostinato [It.] (ah-stee-NAH-toh) - A repeated pattern used as a harmonic basis.

optional divisi (opt. div.) [It.] (dee-VEE-see) - The part splits into optional harmony. The smaller sized *cued notes* indicate the optional notes to be used.

pastorale - Subject matter pertaining to nature (outdoor) scenes.

pesante [It.] (peh-SAHN-teh) - With emphasis.

phrase marking (⌒ **)** - An indication by either the *composer* or the *arranger* as to the length of a line of music or melody. This marking often means that the musician is not to breathe during its duration. See also *no breath.*

piano (*p*) [It.] (pee-AH-noh) - Soft.

pianissimo (*pp*) [It.] (pee-ah-NEE-see-moh) - Very soft.

pianississimo (*ppp*)[It.] (pyah-nees-SEES-see-moh) - Very, very soft. The softest common dynamic marking.

pick-up - An incomplete measure at the beginning of a song or phrase.

pitch - The highness or lowness of musical sounds.

più [It.] (pew) - More. (Ex. più forte or più mosso allegro)

plainsong - An ancient liturgical (sacred) chant–a single melody line with free rhythm sung *a cappella.*

poco [It.] (POH-koh) - Little. (Ex. poco cresc. = a little crescendo)

poco a poco [It.] (POH-koh ah POH-koh) - Little by little (Ex. poco a poco cresc. = increase in volume, little by little)

polyphonic - See polophony.

polyphony [Gr.] (paw-LIH-faw-nee) - Music which consist of two or more independent melodies which combine to create simultaneous voice parts with different rhythms. Polyphony often involves contrasting dynamics and imitation from part to part. From the Greek words meaning "many sounds," polyphony is sometimes called counterpoint.

polyrhythm - Contrasting rhythms played simultaneously.

prestissimo [It.] (pres-tees-see-moh) - Faster than *presto.* As fast as possible.

presto [It.] (PREH-stoh) - Very fast.

quasi [L.] - Seemingly, or in a sense or manner.

rallentando (*rall.*) [It.] (rahl-en-TAHN-doh) - Gradually slower. See also *ritardando.*

refrain - The *chorus* of a song, usually repeated.

relative major/minor - Major and minor tonalities which share the same *key signature.*

Renaissance Period (ca. 1450-1600) (REHN-neh-sahns) - A period in the Western world following the Middle Ages. Renaissance means "rebirth" and was a celebration of entrance into the modern age of thought and invention. In music it was a period of great advancement in notation and compositional ideas. *Polyphony* was developing and the *madrigal* became popular. Orlando di Lasso, Giovanni da Palestrina, Tomás Luis de Victoria, and Josquin Des Prez were some of the more famous Renaissance composers.

repeat sign (𝄆 𝄇) - Repeat the section. If the repeat sign is omitted, go back to the beginning. See also *endings*.

resolution (res.) - A progression from a dissonant tone or harmony to a consonant harmony. (Usually approached by step.) See also *suspension.*

rhythm - The organization of non-pitched sounds in time. Rhythm encompasses note and rest duration as well as *meters, tempos,* and their relationships.

ritardando (*rit.*) [It.] (ree-tahr-DAHN-doh) - Gradually slower. See also *rallentando.*

ritenuto [It.] (rih-teh-NOO-toh) - Slowed down. Usually more abrupt than a *ritardando* or *rallentando.*

ritmico [It.] (riht-MEE-koh) - Rhythmic.

Romantic Period (ca. 1825-1900) - A period in 19th century Western art, literature, and music that lasted into the early 20th century. In music, as well as the other areas, Romanticism focused on the emotion of art. Works from this period emphasized the emotional effect music has on the listener through dynamic contrasts and different ways of changing the "mood." Opera flourished as well as chamber music. Some famous Romantic composers are Franz Schubert, Frederick Chopin, Hector Berlioz, Johannes Brahms, and Richard Wagner.

root tone - The lowest note of a *triad* in its original position; the note on which the chord is built and named.

round - see *canon.*

rubato [It.] (roo-BAH-toh) - The tempo is free, left up to the interpretation of the director or performer.

scale - An inventory or collection of pitches. The word "scale" (from the Italian *scala*) means ladder. Thus, many musical scales are a succession of pitches higher and lower.

score - The arrangement of a group of vocal and instrumental staffs which all sound at the same time.

sempre [It.] (SEHM-preh) - Always , continually. (Ex. sempre forte = always loud)

senza [It.] (SEN-tsah) - Without.

sequence - The successive repetition of a short melodic idea at different pitch levels.

sforzando, sforzato (*sfz*, *sf*) [It.] (sfor-TSAHN-doh, sfor-TSAH-toh) - A strong accent on a note.

sfp (*sfp*) [It.] - Abbr. for *sforzando* followed immediately by *piano,* i.e., a sudden loud *accent* followed immediately by a soft continuation.

sharp (♯) - An *accidental* that raises the pitch of a note one half step. Also, faulty intonation in which the note is sung slightly above the correct pitch.

sign (𝄋 or Segno) [It.] (SEHN-yoh) - A symbol that marks the place in music where the musician is to skip back to from the *dal Segno* (*D.S.*).

simile (*sim.*) [It.] (SIM-eh-lee) - Continue the same way.

simple meter - Meters which are based upon the note which receives the beat. (Ex. $\frac{4}{4}$ or **𝄴** is based upon the quarter note receiving the beat.)

skip - The melodic movement of one note to another in *intervals* larger than a step.

slide (⁄♩) - To approach a note from underneath the designated pitch and "slide" up to the correct pitch. Slides often appear in jazz, pop tunes, and *spirituals.*

slur (𝅗𝅥⁀♩) - A curved line placed above or below a group of notes to indicate that they are to be sung on the same text syllable. Slurs are also used in instrumental music to indicate that the group of notes should be performed *legato* (smoothly connected).

smear - A slide into a note from below. Used often in pop or jazz styles of music. See *slide.*

solfège [Fr.] (SOHL-fehj) - The study of sight-singing using pitch syllables (do re mi, etc.).

soli [It., Lat., Sp.] (SOH-lee) - A section that performs alone or as a predominant part.

solo [It., Lat., Sp.] (SOH-loh] - Alone. To perform alone or as a predominant part.

song cycle - A group of songs, usually for solo voice and piano, constituting a literary and musical unit. Often the poems of a song cycle are by the same poet.

soprano - The highest treble voice, usually written in *treble clef.*

sostenuto [It.] (saws-teh-NOO-toh) - Sustained. Often implying a slowing of tempo.

spirito [It.] (SPEE-ree-toh) - Spirit.

spiritoso [It.] (spee-ree-TOH-soh) - Spirited.

spiritual - Religious folk songs of African American origin associated with work, recreation, or religious gatherings. They developed prior to the Civil War and are still influential today. They have a strong rhythmic character and are often structured in *call and response.*

spoken - Reciting text with the speaking voice rather than singing the designated line. Often indicated with instead of notes.

staccato ( )[It.] (stah-KAH-toh) Short, separated notes. Opposite of *legato.*

staff - The five horizontal parallel lines and four spaces between them on which notes are placed to show *pitch.* The staff can be extended by using *ledger lines.*

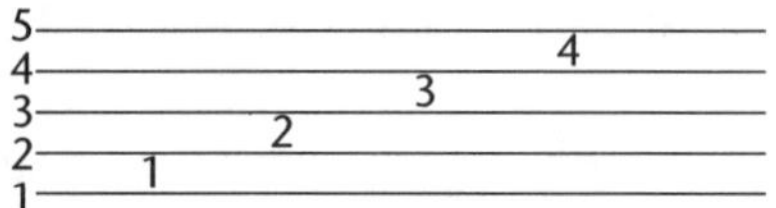

The lines and spaces are numbered from the bottom up.

staggered breathing - In ensemble singing, planning the breaths so that no two singers take a breath at the same time, thus creating the overall effect of continuous singing.

step - Melodic movement from one note to the next higher or lower *scale* degree.

strophe - A strophe is a verse or stanza in a song. If a song has many verses it is said to be strophic.

strophic - A song in which all verse are sung to the same music.

style marking - An indicator at the beginning of a song or section of song which tells the musician, in general, what style the music should be performed. (Ex. *freely* or *animato*)

subdominant chord (abbreviated IV) - The name of the triad built on the fourth degree of the major scale. Subdominant is also a category of harmony that evokes a feeling of degression or diversion away from the *tonic.*

subito (*sub.*) [It.] (SOO-bee-toh) - Suddenly. (Ex. sub. piano = suddenly soft)

submediant chord (abbreviated vi) - The name of the triad built on the sixth degree of the major scale—below the *tonic,* midway between it and the *dominant.*

supertonic chord (abbreviated ii) - The name of the triad built on the second degree of the major scale—immediately above the *tonic chord.*

suspension (sus.) - The sustaining or "suspending" of a pitch from a consonant chord into a dissonant chord often using a *tie.* The resulting dissonant chord then *resolves* to a consonant chord. The musical effect is one of tension and release. See also *resolution.*

swing - A change in interpretation of eighth note durations in some music (often jazz and *blues*). Groups of two eighth notes ( ) are no longer sung evenly, instead they are performed like part of a *triplet* ( ). The eighth notes still appear . A swing style is usually indicated at the beginning of a song or section (=).

syllables - Names given to pitch units or rhythm units to aid in sight-reading.

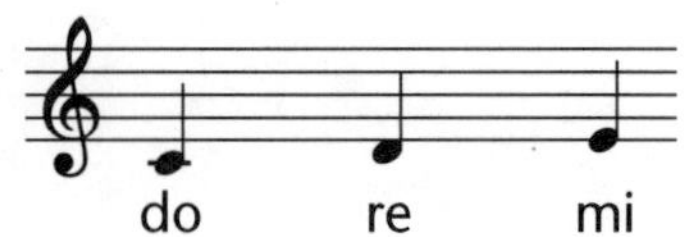

ta	ta	ti	ti	ta
1	2	3	&	4

syncopation - The use of *accents* and *ties* to create rhythmic interest. The result is a rhythmic pattern which stresses notes on the off beat. This technique is commonly found in *spirituals* and jazz.

tempo - The speed of the beat.

tempo marking [It.] - The speed at which music is performed. For example, (♩ = 80) indicates that the speed of the music is to be 80 *beats* per minute.

tempo I - Return to the first tempo. Also called tempo primo.

tempo primo [It.] (TEHM-poh PREE-moh) - Return to the first (*primo*) tempo. See *Tempo I.*

tenor - A male voice written in *bass clef* or *treble clef.* It is lower than the *alto*, but higher than the *bass.*

tenuto (𝅘𝅥) [It.] (teh-NOO-toh) - A slight stress on the indicated note. The note is held for its full value.

terraced dynamics - A technique commonly found in *Baroque* music in which dynamic changes are made suddenly (for example *p* (piano) and suddenly *f* (forte)).

text painting - The musical illustration of the meaning of words in vocal music, especially the literal meaning of individual words or phrases. For example, to create an image of a lonesome prairie, the composer may use a *legato* musical line, word inflection and long phrases to paint the picture for the listener.

texture - The interrelationship of the voices and/or instruments within a piece of music. *Monophonic, homophonic,* and *polyphonic* are all types of textures.

tie (𝅘𝅥‿𝅗𝅥) - A line connecting two or more notes of the same pitch so that their durations are their combined sum. Ties often occur over *barlines.*

time signature - The symbol placed at the beginning of a composition or section to indicate its meter. This most often takes the form of a fraction ($\frac{4}{4}$ or $\frac{3}{4}$), but may also involve a symbol as in the case of common time (𝄴) and cut time (𝄵). The upper number indicates the number of beats in a measure and the lower number indicates which type of note receives the beat. (An exception occurs in *compound meters.* See *compound meter* for an explanation.)

to coda - Go to the 𝄌 .

tonality - The organization of *pitches* in a song in which a certain pitch (tone) is designated as the *key-note* or the note which is the tonal center of a *key.*

tone - A musical sound of definite pitch and quality.

tonic - The *key-note* of a key or scale.

tonic chord (abbreviated I) - The name of the triad built on the first degree (or *keynote*) of the major scale. Tonic is also a category of harmony that evokes a feeling of home or rest.

transpose - To rewrite or perform a song in a *key* other than the original.

treble clef - The symbol at the beginning of the staff used for higher voices and instruments, and the piano right hand. It generally refers to pitches higher then *middle* C. The curve is wrapped around the G, as a result it is also called the G clef.

triad - A special type of 3-note chord built in 3rds over a *root tone.*

trill (*tr* ~~~~) - Rapid alteration (within a key) between the marked note and the one above it.

triple - Any *time signature* or group of beats that is a multiple of 3.

triplet - A borrowed division of the beat where three notes of equal duration are to be sung in the time normally occupied by two notes of equal duration. Usually indicated with a 3.

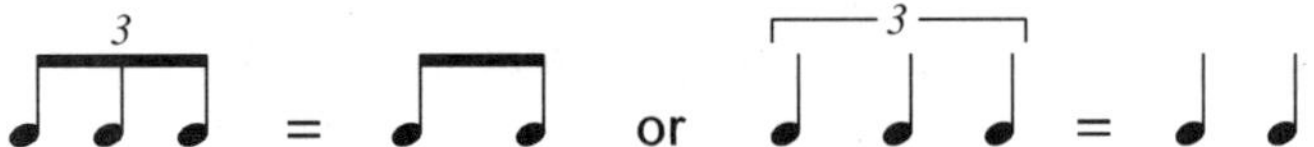

tutti [It.] (TOO-tee) - From the Italian word for "all." *Tutti* is an indicator following a solo or small ensemble that the entire section should all sing.

unison (unis.) - All parts singing the same notes at the same time (or singing in *octaves*).

vivace [It.] (vee-VAH-cheh) - Very fast.

whole step - The combination of two successive half steps. Shown symbolically (⊔).

TO THE TEACHER

Why We Wrote This Book

We created this series because we are vitally committed to the nurturing of choral music, to the more effective teaching of choral music, and particularly to the encouragement of all young people who perform choral music. We believe that each person is musically expressive and deserves the opportunity to explore that capacity.

Too often, our definitions of literacy have been limited to words on paper. Although aspects of music can be taught as the written word (i.e., as a series of facts or as a written symbolic language), ultimately music is perhaps not best understood through the written word, but rather as a unique way of looking at the world, a special dimension of human understanding. What one understands, expresses, or feels when performing choral music is indeed "another way of knowing." We believe that it is vital that all persons be given opportunities to experience this expanded literacy.

About the Series

Essential Elements for Choir consists of two different components – the Music and the Method – on four different levels of difficulty.

THE MUSIC

Essential Elements for Choir for Mixed, Treble, and Tenor Bass Voices • Levels 1-4

These anthologies, targeted for grades 6-12, contain choral literature especially selected for choirs of differing ages and levels of experience. A wide range of repertoire is included in each book:

- a variety of historical periods represented
- a variety of folk songs from other countries and cultures
- a mixture of English and foreign-language texts
- a variety of beginning level and more challenging level songs
- a mixture of styles: masterworks, folk songs, contemporary compositions and spirituals; a cappella and accompanied pieces; sacred and secular works; arrangements of familiar songs and more.

For each level there are three different books: Mixed Voices, Treble Voices, and Tenor Bass Voices. The one exception to this practice is Level 1 which provides only one book written for two- and three-part voices. The music selection is different for every book in an attempt to provide the best literature available for a particular voicing and level of difficulty.

- **Level 1 for Two- and Three-Part Voices**
  For the beginning or inexperienced choir. Although written with upper elementary and middle school in mind, this book may be used in any beginning situation. The literature includes rounds, unison, two-part, and some three-part songs.
- **Level 2 for Mixed, Treble, or Tenor Bass Voices**
  For the choir with limited experience. The music selections take into account the characteristics of the adolescent voice with special consideration to vocal range and age appropriateness. These books are intended for use in the middle school and/or beginning high school choirs.
- **Level 3 for Mixed, Treble, or Tenor Bass Voices**
  For the advanced choir with choral experience. The majority of the music in Level 3 is written for 3- or 4-part choirs. The literature is appropriate for high school level ensembles or other experienced groups.
- **Level 4 for Mixed, Treble, or Tenor Bass Voices**
  For the very advanced choral ensemble. The literature on this level is appropriate for high school, college, or other highly experienced choirs.

Student Components

Each song is treated as an independent unit of study. Prior to each song is a page of information to be read by the student. Student lessons consist of:

- Title and Composer, text and voicing information
- Cultural/Historical Context of song
- Musical Terms and concepts (All terms are listed in the glossary at the back of the book.)
- Preparation activities
- Evaluation activities
- The complete song

Teacher Components

Each teacher edition is spiral bound for easy use at the piano and also contains a full glossary of terms. The individual teacher lessons contain the following:

- Student Text Pages (slightly reduced in size)
- Vocal Ranges and song information at a glance (key, meter, form, programming suggestions, etc.)
- Learning Objectives based on the National Standards for Arts Education
- Historical/Stylistic Guidelines
- Vocal Technique/Warm-ups/Exercises
- Rehearsal Guidelines with Suggested Teaching Sequence
- Performance Tips
- Evaluation suggestions for assessing student progress on the stated objectives
- Extension activities
- The complete song

Choral directors who are just entering the profession or those who have limited skills in teaching choral music are encouraged to follow the suggested Rehearsal Guidelines as written. Experienced choral directors may want to refer to the Performance Tips for ideas on how other experienced directors approach and refine a piece of music. The Evaluation activities provide practical, yet innovative ways to assess student achievement.

Performance/Accompaniment/Part-Learning CD Paks

Every song in *Essential Elements for Choir for Mixed, Treble, and Tenor Bass Voices • Levels 1-4* is recorded three ways: 1. Full Performance, 2. Accompaniment only, 3. Individual Part-Learning.

THE METHOD

Essential Elements for Choir – Musicianship • Levels 1-4

With these books, the choral director has access to a comprehensive musicianship curriculum that can be used in the choral classroom. The material, presented in a practical and sequential manner, covers the areas of *vocal technique, music theory, sight-reading* and *ensemble performance.* It is intended that the Musicianship books be used during the first 10-15 minutes of every choir rehearsal to improve musical skills. Daily use of these books will produce amazing results!

- **Level 1**
  A basic primer that introduces the staff, notation, rhythm, and simple sight-reading skills. Although intended for use by the upper elementary chorus, any beginning choral ensemble may use this book. Exercises and songs are written in treble and bass clefs.
- **Level 2**
  Begins with a review of the basic material presented in Book 1, but then moves forward at a faster rate. It is recommended for the middle school chorus or beginning high school program.
- **Level 3**
  Contains review material from Book 2, but again moves forward at a much faster pace. The practice songs are written for 3- and 4- parts choruses. This book is intended for the average high school chorus.
- **Level 4**
  Is intended for the advanced choir that has successfully completed the three previous books.

TEACHER RESOURCE KIT

This resource book contains reproducible student activity pages on the subjects of voice development, music theory, melodic and rhythmic reading, rehearsal and performance techniques, concert etiquette, music listening, music history, and music activities linked to other subject areas in the curriculum. Assessment tools are provided in the form of charts, checklists, quizzes, writing activities, listening lessons and more.

In Conclusion

Essential Elements for Choir for Mixed, Treble and Tenor Bass Voices along with the *Essential Elements for Choir - Musicianship* books serve as a complete curriculum for the choral experience – a core library of repertoire aimed at awakening the singer's potential for self-development, musical expression, and personal esteem.